# To Be a Presbyterian

*Revised Edition*

# To Be a Presbyterian

## Revised Edition

## Louis B. Weeks

Geneva Press
Louisville, Kentucky

*First published by John Knox Press, 1983*

*Revised edition*
Published by Geneva Press
Louisville, Kentucky

10 11 12 13 14 15 16 17 18 19—10 9 8 7 6 5 4 3 2 1

Grateful acknowledgment is made to the members and ministers of Anchorage Presbyterian Church whose names and words appear in this study.

*Book design by Sharon Adams*
*Cover design by Night & Day Design*
*Cover illustration: gettyimages/photographer: UpperCut Images*

**Library of Congress Cataloging-in-Publication Data**

Weeks, Louis.
  To be a Presbyterian / Louis B. Weeks. — Rev. ed.
      p. cm.
  Includes bibliographical references.
  ISBN 978-0-664-50301-7 (alk. paper)
  1. Presbyterian Church.   I. Title.
  BX9175.3.W44   2010
  285'.1—dc22
                                2009028320

*For Carolyn, Lou, Lillian, Calvin, Abigail,*
*Sid, Youko, Grace, Louis, and James*

# Contents

# Introduction

Peggy Cunningham asked a straight question: "What does it mean to be a Presbyterian?" I tried to give a straight answer. I promised to tell her and the other members of the Issues Class at Anchorage Presbyterian Church in Louisville, Kentucky, about some distinctive emphases of Reformed theology and about Presbyterian styles of church government.

Actually, Peggy Cunningham had a good understanding of what Presbyterians believe, but she had not grown up as one, and she lacked confidence in her knowledge. After class, she and her husband, Bill, said they both would appreciate a study of the church they had joined as adults.

"My cousins and uncles were Buddhists as I grew up," Peggy explained. "I joined the Congregational Church because they kept up a dialogue with the other living religions. After I moved from Honolulu, Hawaii, to the mainland, we belonged to several different denominations. We joined here because this church tries to help those in need, and the worship suits our faith."

From that conversation thirty years ago in one congregation, where Peggy Cunningham and I shared worship and work at the time, I wrote a book for new members in Presbyterian congregations. Published in 1983, months before the joining of northern and southern branches to form the current Presbyterian Church

(U.S.A.), the book anticipated the new denomination and sought to address both its theology and practice succinctly.

The first edition of *To Be a Presbyterian*—used widely in new-member classes, officer training sessions, adult classes, and youth group meetings—proved helpful and provocative. As the PC(USA) came together, I was drawn into conversations with many others asking Peggy's question. Over time I was asked to teach and preach among Presbyterians in every part of the country. Small congregations, big ones, men's gatherings, women's meetings, synod and presbytery workshops—all contributed to my education. I also visited Presbyterian churches in other parts of the world—Ghana, Korea, Scotland, Canada, and France. As I kept learning, I came to appreciate even more the special contributions Presbyterians make to the whole Christian family.

In the late 1980s, colleagues and I received the first of several grants to analyze American Presbyterians as a case study of mainstream Protestants in the twentieth century. We edited six volumes and wrote two more ourselves as a result of our work and that of seventy others who provided essays on many topics— our hymns, our missionary efforts, our finances, our schools, our organization, our evangelism, and many more. You might enjoy reading some of them, studies in the series The Presbyterian Presence: The Twentieth-Century Experience (1990– 1992) and *Vital Signs: The Promise of Mainstream Protestantism* (1996, 2002).

We learned much working together, listening to Presbyterians who were new Christians, sixth-generation Presbyterians, and people who became Presbyterians from a wide range of other religious perspectives. So it made sense to revisit this subject for new Presbyterians and all those interested in our life together. For a while, however, I was too busy helping lead Union Seminary in Virginia, then Union-PSCE, then Union-PSCE in Richmond and Charlotte, for in my time there we merged two schools and opened a new campus in the Carolinas. In thirty years my perspective has changed concerning what we need to know to be good Christians in a particular Presbyterian congregation.

And the Presbyterian churches and the denomination itself have changed considerably since 1983 as well.

Much of the teaching of the first edition is still true, but additional sections and chapters treat subjects important for Presbyterians today that were not "on our radar" thirty years ago.

I use some of the illustrations from the original edition as well. After Anchorage Presbyterian outside Louisville, Kentucky, my home church became the Highland Presbyterian Church in that city. When my wife and I moved to Richmond, Virginia, in 1994, home was the Ginter Park Presbyterian Church, a congregation begun by the faculty and students of the seminary I served. Now in retirement we live in Williamsburg, Virginia, and Carolyn is on the session of the Williamsburg Presbyterian Church, as she had served on the sessions of the Anchorage and Ginter Park congregations when we lived in Louisville and Richmond. Some illustrations come from these churches, and still others from the hundreds of churches in which I have taught, preached, and worshiped along the way.

I hope that this new edition of *To Be a Presbyterian*, while somewhat longer, can be succinct as well. I hope it helps you grow in faith. I hope it answers some questions for you while raising others. And I hope you enjoy seeing and hearing of other Presbyterians as they too seek to be faithful Christians in a world that desperately needs good witnesses to the gospel of Jesus Christ.

## The Faith Pilgrimage

If you did not grow up as a Presbyterian, you are in the majority, along with Peggy Cunningham. Fewer than 40 percent of those in the Presbyterian Church (U.S.A.) today were born into the church. Most Presbyterians were born into other parts of the Christian family. (Carolyn, for example, grew up in the United Methodist Church.) Increasing numbers of Presbyterians come from what we joke to be the "NRP Church" (No Religious Preference). Many, as Peggy Cunningham, have come from others of the living religions, and many more Presbyterians enjoy sports

and practices, such as yoga, karate, and transcendental medita-
tion, from those traditions.

People become and remain Presbyterians for a whole range of
different reasons. We like the minister. Good friends belong to
the local Presbyterian church. Someone from the church helped
us in a time of crisis. We want to help other people, and we find
the local church an effective place to serve. We also find many
like-minded people, frequently ignorant about the specific history and nature of the Presbyterian Church but eager to be good
Christians all the same.

As I teach and preach in different congregations across the
country, I like to ask about the religious pilgrimage of Presbyterians. One young man in the Glen Avon Presbyterian Church
in Duluth, Minnesota, still takes the prize for frankness. "I just
joined this church because my wife had begun coming here," he
told me. "I wanted our kids to be raised with good values."

He wondered aloud if some book would help explain the beliefs
of Presbyterians. I suggested the Bible, and we laughed together.
Now he may have been excessively modest about his own faith,
but many Presbyterians share his expressed reason for being in
the church.

Years ago I began asking in Presbyterian groups about the pilgrimage of each member. The results are usually fascinating, and
frequently someone will thank me for asking. When I began asking in the early 1970s, people frequently apologized if they had
not been reared Presbyterian. "Everyone here seems to assume
all of us have always been Presbyterian!" someone would exclaim.
"I'm sorry, but I was Catholic." Today, by contrast, people seem
to brag about the variety and extent of their pilgrimage. "I was
raised Baptist, spent three years in an ashram, and now I belong
here and also study Bible with the Lutherans."

From our research for the Presbyterian Presence series, my
colleagues and I found that few people today join the Presbyterian Church (U.S.A.). People join First Presbyterian Church
in Shreveport, Louisiana; Little River Presbyterian Church in
Hurdles Mills, North Carolina; or Second Presbyterian Church
in Indianapolis. They join a local congregation. Incidentally, we

found that if they were to leave, they would quit almost always for local reasons—a dramatic contrast with earlier periods in American history when people felt denominational loyalty and when they moved would find a church from the same denomination.

No wonder it is difficult in most congregations, indeed in many sessions, to assume that knowledge of our Presbyterian tradition is a shared perspective. In a seminar in Muskingum Valley Presbytery in Ohio, an older minister said with humor and some sadness, "I kept quoting John Calvin, and after several years I guess somebody got up the courage to say after worship one day, 'Who is this John Calvin, anyway?'" Another minister chimed in that she had discovered many people could not follow her when she used words like "regeneration" and "sanctification."

Of course, Presbyterians, at least in the United States, never enjoyed "good old days" when everyone knew the tradition and lived it. In every generation, Presbyterians have struggled with worship and work, ethical matters and biblical interpretation.

Actually there may be more serious reading of the Bible today than in previous generations. Many Presbyterian seminaries since the 1960s, for the first time in American history, require a reading of *Institutes of the Christian Religion*, the work by Calvin on which much Reformed theology has been based.

A few generations ago, Presbyterian seminarians came mostly from Presbyterian families, and they had learned one particular interpretation of Calvinism through exclusive attention to the Westminster Confession of Faith and its Larger and Shorter Catechisms from the 1640s. These "Westminster Standards," still important for us, were the major curriculum for Christian education among Presbyterians in nineteenth-century America. Before that, in the eighteenth century, few Presbyterians possessed more than three books—usually the Bible, John Foxe's *Book of Martyrs*, which tells of Protestants who suffered and died for their faith, and a copy of the Westminster Standards. This heritage meant a rather tightly constructed worldview was part of the experience of most Presbyterians, and those who could read the Bible centered upon it through these eyes.

When the United Presbyterian Church U.S.A., the so-called northern church, adopted its Confession of 1967, it also adopted a *Book of Confessions* that maintained the Westminster Standards and included as well Reformed creeds from other parts of the tradition. In 1991 the PC(USA) General Assembly, now eight years old, adopted a "Brief Statement of Reformed Faith" and retained the *Book of Confessions.*

Today, many more sources of information are available to us. Newspapers, television, and Internet resources present worldviews that differ greatly from traditional Presbyterian perspectives. The ecumenical movement also brings many varieties of Christian belief to bear on the lives of Presbyterians. Works of fiction, both in literature and movies, results of the social and natural sciences—all bombard our senses with important and worthwhile instruction (as well as with much drivel that needs to be ignored). The very learning that can help in mutual understanding and the gaining of wisdom can also interfere with the transmission of tradition.

## Questions for the Study

We are not necessarily better or worse off than Presbyterians of previous generations. People and leaders in the churches are asking with increasing frequency for honest and useful presentations of basic beliefs. What do people "have to believe" to be Presbyterians? What are the beliefs necessary in order to be a leader in the church, an elder or a minister? What other beliefs are important but not essential in Reformed communions?

In perhaps even more profound ways, people ask about the meaning of Presbyterian beliefs for Christian living. What practices and ethical stances do Presbyterians share with all the rest of Christ's body? Are there distinctive or unique beliefs and practices among Presbyterians? How does the theology of the church relate to the salvation of people? What do the authority of the Bible and the tradition affirmed mean in everyday human situations? How do beliefs about God, Jesus Christ, the Spirit, and the church affect values and decision making?

These questions, and others like these, are phrased frequently in term of comparison: "What is the difference between Baptists and Presbyterians on the Lord's Supper?" Sometimes they are not phrased as questions at all: "I think this congregation should have more meetings and decide the important things for the church by majority vote, the way we did at Community Church!"

Most Presbyterians want honestly to be faithful in their allegiance to Jesus Christ and their commitment to the church. They seek to know the implications of their Presbyterian affiliation.

This study is intended as a response to questions and statements such as these by people in local churches. I write for folks who did not grow up learning the Children's Catechism, those who have not made their way through the Westminster Standards or Calvin's *Institutes*, and those who have not studied the other creeds that form part of the Reformed tradition in the United States. The work is meant primarily for adults, but creative teachers can easily use it with younger, confirmation-age Christians.

I believe strongly that Presbyterians have had a special presence in America and have particular contributions to make in our society. I grant the same convictions from Catholics, Lutherans, Baptists, Greek Orthodox, and others. As a Presbyterian, I draw on a tradition that offers me food and drink both nourishing and appetizing. I am delighted whenever I have the opportunity to share this hearty diet with other people. By the same token, I know and enjoy the fact that every Christian does not exist and thrive on this Reformed diet. I eagerly hear and worship with those of other traditions.

The wider faith, beyond and beneath our particular faiths, does remain primary. No study of Presbyterianism can ignore the vast area of common faith and action. In this age of denominational mobility and ecumenical cooperation, we just assume the sharing of the Christian responsibility to feed the hungry, clothe the naked, and care for the needy (Matt. 25:35–36). We assume also the shared call to "make disciples of all nations" (Matt. 28:19). We hear together the promises of Jesus, and we together pray for God's kingdom to come "on earth, as it is in heaven" (Matt. 6:10).

By the same token, I see real problems for people who do not orient their faith in a particular portion of the Christian tradition. My friend Syngman Rhee, recently moderator of the PC(USA), says such folk are like "cut flowers" that may look pretty for a brief time but have no roots to endure and flourish. The heritage of every Christian includes all of church history. Among the mixed elements of this heritage, each of us claims a part as tradition, actively informing our lives.

In the United States today, many of us are tempted simply not to claim a particular tradition. The whole heritage has merely washed over us. We define ourselves vaguely as "Protestant Christians." The better definition might be "vaguely religious." How much better it would be if people who want to be Christian maintain the health and vitality of a particular tradition!

I find the Reformed tradition a good place on which to stand. From its perspective other traditions make sense, and I can see merits in almost all of them. Thus this study is written from an ecumenical, but also especially from a Reformed, point of view. When tragedy has struck close to me, Presbyterian tradition has offered an avenue of real Christian solace. When world events seem out of control, or when I am tempted to doubt God's care or justice, Reformed faith has stood me in good stead. I see God's promise in it for the believer, for the church universal, and for the whole creation. But always the Reformed version of God's promise comes as a portion of the full Christian faith that supersedes all Christian traditions.

## Basic Outline

This study begins with very basic beliefs of Presbyterians—those required for membership in the denomination. Presbyterians are Christians first and last. We believe with Simon, renamed Peter, that Jesus is Christ, "the Son of the living God" (Matt. 16:16). We trust God, the creator and provider of all good things. We believe with the apostle Paul that "God was in Christ, reconciling the world to himself" (2 Cor. 5:19). And we believe Christ's Spirit, the Holy Spirit, is sustaining us all in Christian life, giving us God's gifts through all our lives. The first four chapters tell about these basic beliefs and the ways in which we have received them.

Chapters 5 through 8 describe the ways in which Presbyterians have focused in particular fashion on their religious life. Traditional piety and ethics have been hallmarks of Reformed life, involving the whole person in service to God and to neighbors. "What does the LORD require of you," the prophet Micah asked, "but to do justice, and to love kindness, and to walk humbly with your God?" (Mic. 6:8). At the same time, Presbyterians have celebrated the sacraments of the Lord's Supper and baptism as a portion of the Christian response to God's work in Christ. Again, the understanding of the work of these sacraments has retained a distinctive flavor in Presbyterian churches.

Chapters 9 through 12 tell some things about citizenship in the Reformed church family. What does it mean to participate responsibly in the church itself? What of the society of which the Christian is part? How are Presbyterians members of the "communion of saints"?

The final three chapters are new, prompted by questions from those who read and discussed the first edition with me and by recent events and insights.

The divisions in this study, although rather traditional, are nevertheless arbitrary. The main characteristic of classical Reformed faith has been that everything fits together in a whole. The Reformed perspective on the Christian faith does not collect a group of different ideas and experiences and try to fit them together. On the contrary, Presbyterians celebrate the creative and purposeful work of God as we have come to know it in Christ Jesus, by the grace of the Spirit. We in turn live creatively and purposefully in all we are and all we do, both in church and in work, in play and in prayer. In the words of Paul, "We know that in everything God works for good with those who love him, who are called according to his purpose" (Rom. 8:28). At several points this particular theme will recur, for in our complex and often fragmented world, demonic forces pull us away from this center of God's wholeness.

One final introductory note: the illustrations in this book come from actual people and churches. Most of the examples come from congregations in which my family and I have participated. My choice of real people and historical events is partly from habit, because I teach church history. But I like to think it comes mainly from Reformed theology. In our affirmation of the "priesthood of believers," we say in effect that we intercede with one another before God. We teach each other about God's care and forgiveness, about living in the world and anticipating God's kingdom. We all learn through the lives and work of others, and I seek to turn our attention to that process wherever possible.

My choice of illustrations also relates to the ways in which this study will be most useful for groups, classes, and individuals. Try to think of your situation as you read about and discuss the various topics. As I have mentioned Peggy Cunningham, who grew up in Hawaii, you may think of other persons of quite different backgrounds. As I talk about ministers in local congregations, I hope you will make a definite translation into your own circumstances. As I give examples about the decisions others make and the prayers they pray, I hope you will be thinking about your own. The more these various subjects can be related to your own Christian faith and life, the more helpful the study will be.

## Chapter One

# To Be a Christian

Scores of us gather in Williamsburg on September 11 for an ecumenical prayer service. We remember the victims, their families, and all those who have died, lost loved ones, and become refugees in the aftermath of the suicide strikes on the World Trade Center and the Pentagon, the crash of the third plane in Pennsylvania, and the subsequent wars in Afghanistan and Iraq. Our pastor, Patrick Willson, shares in leading the worship. So does Jim Weaver, our director of music, who leads a joint choir of Catholics, Lutherans, Baptists, Methodists, and Episcopalians from nine congregations. The choir sings a haunting Kyrie, "Year That Trembled and Reeled beneath Me."

We gather in the St. Bede Catholic Church this year—Christians from all over town—singing, praying, listening to and reading Scripture, remembering, and hoping together. St. Bede and Williamsburg Presbyterian, where I worship, are "covenant churches" that have promised to pray each week for one another. This ecumenical service is even broader in scope, linking all of the strains of Christian faith in our town that want to be together.

We Presbyterians need to remember how wide and diverse the Christian church really is. We affirm our membership in the one, holy catholic church—the church universal. We confess that truth when we affirm the Apostles' Creed, a formal confession of faith we share with almost all Christians.

1

The Christian community includes people throughout the world whose faith sometimes seems quite different from our own. All these congregations gathered at this service of worship and many more share the Christian faith in this place, doing what Jesus said to do in Matthew 25. We feed the hungry with a joint food pantry, clothe the naked with a clothes closet, visit those in prison with a cooperative ministry, and engage in worship and work together.

The fact that your congregation is part of a worldwide church, a significant part, is the place to begin thinking about what it means to be a Presbyterian. We are Christian believers with Catholics, Orthodox, worshipers in community chapels, members of Pentecostal churches in South America, followers of Christian messianic movements in Africa, and many more strains of the largest religious community on earth—almost one-third of the human family. Further, we claim kinship with the billions of Christians who have preceded us in the faith through all time. To be a Presbyterian, as we remain in the midst of this ecumenical prayer service, is to be a Christian first.

Every congregation I have been part of enjoys special ties with Christians of diverse heritage and theology. At Highland, the links with an African American Baptist church downtown were especially strong. At Ginter Park, the deepest relationships were shared with other congregations in the neighborhood—Methodist, Baptist, and Catholic. Now at Williamsburg Presbyterian, a covenant relationship with a Catholic church in town means we pray for them and they pray for us at every worship service. This past summer, our two congregations held a joint vacation Bible school, open to kids from all over town.

The same is true in every congregation in which I have preached, taught, or studied. Each knows from its work and worship how others of different denominations are equally Christian and deeply committed to the one body of Christ. I honestly believe now that every Presbyterian in this day and time understands and appreciates the diversity within the Christian family.

Catholic, Baptist, Christian (Disciples of Christ), Lutheran, Episcopal, Methodist, and Presbyterian churches cooperate. All of us Protestants should know about that diversity, yet we all share the catholic heritage. The word "catholic" simply means "universal." All Christians call Jesus the Christ.

## A Look at the Family Tree

As Jesus of Nazareth walked, taught, healed people, called disciples, lived, died, and "rose again from the dead," he came to be received by believers as "the Christ, the Son of the living God." People who came to believe that Jesus is the Christ moved from Judaism into a new religious identity related to it. In Antioch (Acts 11:26) they were first called "Christians." Early in their forming process, and following the gospel they had heard and believed, Christians decided that new members of the community did not first have to become Jews, nor did they have to *do* anything else in order to belong. All the doing of God's will had been done in Christ. God's promises revealed that truth also. Jesus the Christ called people to faith. From life in the Spirit flowed new ways of living.

The Acts of the Apostles tells of a time when the whole Christian church was one. "Now the whole group of those who believed were of one heart and soul" (Acts 4:32). One major episode in Acts follows a conference in Jerusalem, when diverse opinions threatened to split the church. Paul, Barnabas, and Peter prevailed to lead the church in settling its argument on requirements for membership. The church, according to that narrative, came to one accord and remained undivided (Acts 15:25).

Quickly, however, the religious organizations of people who followed Jesus Christ developed in different ways. Where persecution occurred, some Christians moved underground and worshiped secretly. Others became bold missionaries and sought to convert their persecutors. Some looked forward to God's kingdom dawning and gave their lives, seeing martyrdom as a step toward that end. Still others, in areas of less overt hostility, tried to explain their new faith in the language of other cultures and philosophies. You can see the variety among Christians as you read the letters to young churches in the New Testament.

The Christian church divided into many parts as time went by. Major splits occurred as leaders considered the nature of the Christ they sought to follow. Every council affirmed an "orthodox" (correct) position, and every council tried to cut off other avenues of talking about and believing in Christ. Through almost all Christian history, different wings of the church have pronounced "anathemas" (curses) on "heresies" (choices) and punished heretics. In our own day, many Christians still jealously guard their own brand of faith as though it were the only one.

Reformed Christians historically have recognized that other communions also bear a portion of God's truth for the world. Frequently, though, when Presbyterians have spoken of "the church," they have meant just their own little congregation or denomination. We do well to remind ourselves that we Presbyterians are just one branch on the Western limb of the Christian family tree. To be specific, Christians in Presbyterian churches are in the Western, Reformed, evangelical tradition. We follow many patterns of the Roman Catholic Church. We hail from the Reformed or "middle" tradition in Protestantism. We consider the gospel to be at the center of our faith. A further word about each of these terms may be helpful.

The Western Church grew from the Latin-speaking Christian communities, with Rome becoming their natural center over time. The Roman Church came to be distinguished from the Eastern, Greek-speaking communities of Christians not only because of language differences but also because the Western Church recognized the Roman bishop as more powerful than the rest. The Eastern, or Orthodox, Church moved gradually to recognize the honorary primacy of the bishop of Constantinople, but each of the self-governing churches in Alexandria, Jerusalem, Antioch, and more recently Russia, Bulgaria, and so forth, possesses great independence from the rest. Another group of "Orthodox" churches separated even further from the Western and even somewhat from the Eastern branches when disagreements occurred about the nature of the Trinity. Those communions, such as the Ethiopian, Syrian, and Armenian, are faithful Christian strains also. But the Presbyterian communions grew from the Western, or Roman Catholic Church, which separated from the Eastern Orthodox Church finally in 1054.

The Western Church has generally called itself "Catholic." During the Middle Ages, leaders in the Western Church tended to grant increasing power to the pope, the bishop of Rome, though many among them argued in behalf of ecumenical councils having the greater power. Proponents of papal power cited the words of Jesus: "You are Peter, and on this rock I will build my church" (Matt. 16:18). Simon Peter received the special authority from Christ to "bind and loose" on earth according to this interpretation, and he became the first bishop of Rome. In the Western Church (as in the Eastern Church), believers were related to God and to the rest of the faithful primarily through the sacraments.

Within the Western Church, critics such as John Wycliffe (1320?–1384) in England and Jan Hus (1374–1415) in Bohemia (Czech Republic) argued that the people were being ignored. Church leaders concentrated on gaining lands and political power under the banner of Rome, while they did not even let common people share in the elements of the Mass. People could not even understand the Latin of the priests or read the Bible in their own languages! Criticism of this system went unheeded by the popes, until the Reformation of the sixteenth century split the Western Christian community. In more recent times, Presbyterians have often forgotten that all of us, Catholic and Protestant, belong to this Western branch of Christianity. St. Bede Catholic Church, our covenant partner at Williamsburg Presbyterian, is a Christian congregation as we are.

### Reformation and Reformed

When Martin Luther (1483–1546) in Germany and Huldrych Zwingli (1484-1531) in Switzerland led protests against the Catholic Church, to which they belonged, various distinct branches of Western Christianity came to have particular identities. At the same time, in the early sixteenth century, Henry VIII, king of England, led a political split from Rome that resulted in a church division. As the Bible became available in various languages for people to read for themselves, more radical interpretations by some resulted in still another, "Anabaptist," movement among Western Christians. From Luther came the Lutheran churches, usually in Europe associated with political governments. From Henry VIII and his successors on the British throne came the Church of England and its offspring in various colonies—one of which eventually became the Episcopal Church in the United States. The Methodist churches also came from Anglican beginnings and went on to form separate denominations late in the eighteenth century. From the Anabaptists came Mennonites, Amish, and Hutterites, and they had some influence on what have become Baptist churches in America. Far more important in starting Baptist communions, and indispensable for what are today Presbyterians, were the Reformed churches, which claimed Zwingli as one early leader.

Reformed leaders such as Zwingli, John Calvin (1510–1564), John Knox (1505–1572), Martin Bucer (1491–1551), and others tried to purify the church morally and to restore it to early patterns of worship and work. They, together with other Protestants, considered faith more important than sacramental ties. Luther had pointed to the promise that Paul references in the Letter to the Romans, that "the one who is righteous will live by faith" (Rom. 1:17, quoting Hab. 2:4). Luther saw in all the Prophets, Law, and Gospels this theme as the core of the Bible's proclamation. If the Bible offered a genuine revelation of God's truth for people, then it should be followed where possible. Though Protestants held many beliefs in common, the Reformed wing came to distinguish itself in several areas of biblical interpretation and church government.

The name "Reformed" evidently appeared first in France. You can see the word chiseled into the wall of the prisons in southern France where "Reformed" martyrs died. By the end of the sixteenth century the word was in general use throughout Europe. From the very beginning, Reformed Christians were not limited to one nation or ethnic group.

American Presbyterians likewise came from many backgrounds. Today the World Alliance of Reformed Churches comprises 75 million Christians in 214 churches in 107 countries, and many Christians of Reformed heritage do not even belong to that body.

## Presbyterians and Congregationalists

The Reformed family of churches includes some that focused upon the passage in which Jesus promises to be "where two or three are gathered in my name" (Matt. 18:20). Some of these Reformed Christians tried to separate themselves from the government of the state in which they lived. Others tried to have their definition of the church become the official one for the people in the realm. Both of these kinds of Reformed Christians belonged to the "Congregationalist" wing of the family, and many Baptists consider themselves "Reformed" in both these streams of tradition.

Presbyterians, on the other hand, sought to include all baptized Christians within the church. Presbyterians paid close attention to the prayer of Jesus that "they may be one," even as he was one with God (John 17:11). Presbyterians advocated representative church government, and they saw the whole church as less prone to err than any particular Christian on his or her own. Presbyterian-type churches became the official religion in Scotland and in portions of the European continent.

As the two wings among Reformed communions grew to distinguish themselves, they continued to cooperate closely in most lands. Their Reformed theology differed little in other respects. John Calvin, whose *Institutes of the Christian Religion* (1536–1559) became a classic statement for Reformed Christians, was claimed by both the Congregationalists and the Presbyterians.

Why are there so few Presbyterians in New England, while they are more numerous in many other parts of the country? In 1801, Congregationalists and Presbyterians agreed that where one Reformed branch already existed, the other would not plant churches. That "Plan of Union," one of the first attempts at "comity," or sharing evangelism in America, did not last forever. But it did make an imprint on Reformed demography to this day.

While this introductory work emphasizes distinctive characteristics of the Reformed churches, it is important to remember that Protestants all share more in doctrine and perspective than they have differences. Since the Second Vatican Council, it seems to me that many Catholics also greatly resemble Protestants in theology and worldview. In fact, the substance of the ecumenical movement affirms today that all together constitute the body of Christ, that all are truly Christians.

### Christians All

Followers of Jesus Christ have always called themselves Christians, at least ever since the believers in Antioch received that name. The label has stuck with the whole body of believers throughout history and has remained the most inclusive designation for the whole church. To be a Christian meant from the very beginning that a person belonged to a community of faith. Christianity began and remains for the most part a corporate religion.

Presbyterians and members of many other branches of the Christian church have tried to continue the tradition of that first community described in the Acts of the Apostles. Part of the life of faith involved listening to the disciples, enjoying fellowship, breaking bread, and praying (Acts 2:42). Early church government consisted in the honoring of each believer and in the selection of leaders from among those with special gifts (Acts 6:1–7). In seeking to restore the spirit of the earliest church, which received the Holy Spirit at Pentecost, Presbyterians and all Reformed Christians did not consider that subsequent Christianity rejected the faith. Reformed Christians admitted that just as all human beings make mistakes, so councils of the church might also err. Nevertheless they affirmed the history of the church and its councils, at least those that formed basic doctrine about the triune nature of God. John Calvin and the rest were quick to affirm the Trinity as an important truth about God.

### "Christians" All

In the sixteenth century, however, some other Protestants who read their Bibles considered the language of the councils at

Nicaea and Chalcedon foreign to the words of Scripture. In the early nineteenth century, Thomas Campbell, his son Alexander Campbell, followers of another ex-Presbyterian named Barton Stone, and some Methodist and Baptist groups said there was no need for the language of Greek philosophy to confuse the simple words of the Bible. They began a movement they called "Christian." Since that time, a number of denominations have grown around the world that call themselves "Christian" and "Church of Christ." The best known of these resulted directly from the merger of the Campbellites and the Stoneites—the Christian Church (Disciples of Christ). To confuse matters further, when the Congregational Christian Church merged with the Evangelical and Reformed Church in 1957, the new Reformed denomination was named "the United Church of Christ." Today, when we Presbyterians identify ourselves as "Christians," many mistake us for members of the Christian Church (Disciples of Christ), United Church of Christ, or another denomination that uses the word in its name. The same holds true for Catholics, Methodists, and Baptists. Just because the word can be misunderstood is no reason to forsake it. In fact, we are all Christians first and foremost; we take our particular denominational names as secondary identities.

## Evangelicals All

We Presbyterians are also almost all evangelicals. We believe that the essence of the faith is the "good news" (*euangelion*) that Jesus Christ lived, died, and rose for us. "God so loved the world that he gave his only Son, that whoever believes in him should not perish but have eternal life" (John 3:16). This gospel is the message we seek to live and to proclaim, as Jesus directed disciples to "go therefore and make disciples of all nations" (Matt. 28:19). This task we enjoy, as do many other kinds of Christians.

In our most recent Presbyterian confession, A Brief Statement of Faith, which was adopted in 1991, we say that "the Spirit gives us courage to pray without ceasing, to witness among all peoples to Christ as Lord and Savior." This evangelical center of faith is common among all the Protestant communions historically, and it characterizes Catholic and Eastern branches increasingly.

In America, Presbyterians have almost always considered Reformed churches to be evangelical in nature. During the nineteenth century, as the voluntary societies such as the American Bible Society, the American Society for Foreign Missions, and the American Tract Society formed, Presbyterians joined with Congregationalists, Methodists, and Baptists to form what they called "the Evangelical United Front." Presbyterians have also led revival movements time and again. In short, Presbyterians have been evangelicals and remain evangelicals.

This point needs to be made in no uncertain terms, because some people in the United States today do not consider Presbyterians to be evangelicals. Just as in the early nineteenth century some Christians claimed that they alone deserved the term "Christian," so in the twentieth century others have said that they alone are "evangelicals." By the same token, many Presbyterians have been critical of the hard-sell tactics and vapid teachings of some so-called evangelicals. But historically and confessionally, Presbyterians have remained evangelicals as surely as we have remained Christians, Protestants, and members of the Reformed family. We have relied on the gospel of Jesus Christ to tell us about the nature of the God we praise.

## Chapter Two

# To Trust God

He's got the whole world, in his hands.
He's got the whole wide world in his hands.

A family night supper one chilly spring evening at Anchorage—I still remember it vividly after some years. Our dinner followed the pattern of a Jewish seder meal. Young people led us in Bible readings and the eating of different symbolic foods. As we sat at various tables around the basement, they led us in singing hymns and Christian songs. We began to clap our hands and sing the rousing spiritual "He's Got the Whole World in His Hands." Elsie Robinson, a stalwart older member of the church whose husband had died just a few months before, bent over toward me and smiled. "Right now," she said, "I know it's true. The world is in God's hands."

To be a Christian, and Elsie Robinson is a good one, means to trust God. Presbyterians emphasize the fact that God gives all the gifts—even the faith to believe in God. In special moments we know, like Elsie Robinson knew, God has the whole world in his hands. "I sought the Lord, and afterward I knew, / He moved my soul to seek him seeking me," is the splendid poem of an anonymous Christian from the nineteenth century. It describes the process of faith in profound truth. To believe in Jesus Christ is to trust God, but we know God gave the Holy Spirit to give us faith and that Jesus Christ is not all there is to God.

Historically, Christians have spoken of God the Father, Son, and Holy Spirit—one God in three persons. Almost every expression explaining what the Trinity means has at some point in the history of the church been considered heretical. But we all agree that God is Creator and provides for all people—indeed, for the whole creation. Brief words about Trinity, creation, providence, and trust are very important, then, in considering basic Presbyterian beliefs and basic Christian beliefs.

## God as Triune

Christians from the very beginning recognized that the relation of Jesus Christ to God was a mystery. Jesus spoke of God sometimes as a being different from himself. In the Gospel according to Luke, for example, we hear that Jesus "spent the night in prayer to God" (6:12). When a rich young man called Jesus "Good Teacher," Jesus replied, "Why do you call me good? No one is good but God alone" (18:18–19). When Jesus died on the cross, according to this Gospel, he cried "with a loud voice," saying, "Father, into your hands I commend my spirit" (23:46).

On other occasions, Jesus said that he and God were almost the same. Speaking among believers and detractors in the Gospel according to John, Jesus said, "Whoever believes in me believes not in me but in him who sent me" (12:44). While praying he said, "The glory that you have given me I have given them [believers] so that they may be one, as we are one" (17:22). Even the preface to that Gospel tells us, "In the beginning was the Word, and the Word was with God, and the Word was God. He was in the beginning with God" (1:1–2).

When Jesus appeared to his disciples as the resurrected one, he said that he would go to be with God and also that he would be with the believers on earth. In the Acts of the Apostles, the writer says that Jesus told his disciples "not to leave Jerusalem, but to wait there for the promise of the Father. . . . 'You will be baptized with the Holy Spirit not many days from now'" (1:4–5).

The Gospel according to Matthew ends with the command of Jesus to his disciples: "Go therefore, and make disciples of all nations, baptizing them in the name of the Father and of the Son and of the Holy Spirit" (28:19).

Very quickly the church developed a doctrine that God was "three in one." This belief became the major point of contention during most of Christian history. The more leaders tried to spell out the meaning of this mystery, especially as it related to the nature of Jesus Christ, the more different traditions emerged. Much of the problem stemmed from the fact that words had different meanings in various parts of the Mediterranean world. Differences among political loyalties and social classes also entered the picture. Many church leaders spoke Greek as a first language, while others used it as a second, trading language. Many others spoke primarily Latin in the Rome-dominated culture. Other more regional languages gave additional flavor to the vocabularies and shades of meaning that differed in various translations.

As they hammered out a theology of the Trinity, Christians kept disagreeing. Church leaders gathered periodically, therefore, for ecumenical (worldwide) assemblies to frame statements of faith. One of the most contested of the definitions of Jesus Christ came in the Council at Nicaea (AD 325), where most of the bishops declared Jesus to be "of one Being with the Father." The exclusion of many Christians who believed that God was high above the transient, changing world and church left scars that have been reopened generation after generation.

When Western leaders gathered more than a century later, they added to the Nicene Creed an assertion that the Holy Spirit "proceeds from the Father and the Son." Eastern leaders considered this an arrogant act on the part of the Rome-based Westerners. In 1254 one pope finally declared that the head of one Eastern Orthodox church would go to hell. The "Great Schism" that resulted continues to plague the Christian church. (See the two versions of the Nicene Creed in *The Presbyterian Hymnal* [1990], page 15.)

While almost everyone's Bible possessed the passage from Matthew, the word "Trinity" itself did not occur. More important, many of the philosophical words used to explain the doctrine were foreign to most Christians.

When Reformed leaders sought to recapture the spirit and the forms of the early church, they did not quarrel with the Western version of the creed, which interpreted the meaning of Trinity. John Calvin, who helped articulate much of the Reformed faith, warned Christians not to dismiss the terms about the Trinity too quickly. We should acknowledge that the doctrines were not rashly invented. By the same token, Calvin declared, we should see how very modestly the great theologians have regarded it. The "modesty of saintly men ought to warn us against forthwith so severely taking to task, like censors, whose who do not wish to swear to the words conceived by us, provided they are not doing it out of either arrogance or forwardness or malicious craft" (*Institutes* 1.13.5).

Subsequently, all of the major Reformed creeds have included the Trinity, but most have been very modest about spelling out the meaning of the mystery. A classic statement of the Trinity can be found in the Westminster Shorter Catechism:

> *How many Persons are there in the Godhead?*
> There are three Persons in the Godhead: the Father, the Son, and the Holy Ghost; and these three are one God, the same in substance, equal in power and glory. (Q.A.6)

The Confession of 1967 says that the Trinity is "recognized and reaffirmed as forming the basis and determining the structure of the Christian faith." It speaks of the work of "God, the Father, Son, and Holy Spirit" (9.07). Our most recent creed, A Brief Statement of Faith, says simply that "we trust in the one triune God, the Holy One of Israel, whom alone we worship and serve" (10.1).

Ninety-nine of a hundred Presbyterians have no difficulty affirming the ancient creeds of the church on the Trinity. The creeds represent the wisdom of early Christians led by the Spirit. Indeed, many Presbyterians can even find in the doctrine of the Trinity a way of meditating on the mystery of God, as Augustine advised many centuries ago. Augustine said analogies exist to help us understand. Notice, he declared, how in a loving relationship among human beings there is a lover, a beloved, and the love itself. All are distinct, but they are one.

I personally consider the historic creeds beautiful, embodying the faith of other generations. They remind us of our duty to share the faith with people throughout the world who use different tongues and face challenges beyond our own. When I was in Ethiopia, I could recognize the point in the worship service at which the Ethiopian Christians said the creed, even though I could not understand the words of the liturgy in Ge'ez and even though they did not say the Roman Catholic version.

What of the Presbyterian who comes from a Baptist or Disciples background, where creeds and the doctrine of the Trinity have been called hindrances to Christian faith? After all, the word "Trinity" itself is not in the Bible. Such traditions, as well as the Christian part of the Unitarian Church, teach that there is a difference between proclaiming God to be Father, Son, and Spirit on one hand, and following the extrascriptural doctrines of Trinity on the other. Can such people be good Presbyterians? The answer seems to be yes.

The *Book of Order* for the Presbyterian Church (U.S.A.) says, "The congregation shall welcome all persons who respond in trust and obedience to God's grace in Jesus Christ and desire to become part of the membership and ministry of his Church" (*Book of Order*, G-5.0103). Again, active members of the church are those who make a profession of faith in Christ, who are baptized, who have submitted to the government of the church, and who participate in the church's life. Baptism, of course, uses the words from Matthew: "in the name of the Father, and of the Son, and of the Holy Spirit." Elders and deacons in the Presbyterian Church do affirm that we will "receive and adopt the essential tenets of the Reformed faith as expressed in the Confessions of our Church." But the regular member has great latitude in belief on this and other matters. After all, if we truly seek to learn about God, Jesus Christ, and about our own responsibilities in the world, we have already moved a great distance along the path of faith. We Trinitarians take such interests as a willingness to learn to be the work of the Spirit, and we recognize the work of God the Father in creation and providence.

## Creator of All

At the bedrock of Reformed faith is the trust in God that God created the universe. God made it all. Presbyterians, who for generations sang mainly metrical versions of the Psalms, have found great joy in hymns such as this:

> O come, let us sing to the LORD;
>> let us make a joyful noise to the rock of our salvation!
> Let us come into his presence with thanksgiving;
>> let us make a joyful noise to him with songs of praise!
> For the LORD is a great God,
>> and a great King above all gods.
> In his hand are the depths of the earth;
>> the heights of the mountains are his also.
> The sea is his, for he made it;
>> and the dry land, which his hands have formed.
>
> Ps. 95:1–5

From Genesis, from the Prophets, from the Wisdom writings as well as from the Psalms, we see the power and love of God expressed in creation. Not only did God make the world, the lands, the seas, the stars, the animals, and human beings, but God also called them all "very good" (Gen. 1:31). It is increasingly appropriate to affirm God's creation of the universe as our knowledge expands concerning its vast stretches and its minute workings. The faith that God made the world and all the rest enables us to praise God, as did the ancient psalmist.

Some Presbyterians honestly believe that God created the whole universe in just six, twenty-four-hour days. Some Presbyterians, myself included, believe that the process of God's creation of the universe began long before the making of life on earth and the fashioning of human beings. I personally see no contradiction between my belief in creation and the theories of evolution that are taught in contemporary scientific disciplines. I am certain, however, that Presbyterians do not have to agree with me on such matters. Nor do I have to agree with the creationists who say dinosaur bones have been placed on earth to test our faith. We all can see how magnificent the creation is, and we can all together praise God for making it (and all of us).

The six-day creationists have words from the confessions to back up their point of view. They can also quote the Westminster Shorter Catechism: "The work of creation is God's making all things of nothing, by the word of his power, in the space of six days, and all very good" (A.9). Some years ago Presbyterians such as I argued that the word "day" signified a long period of time. Today it seems to me better to say that the essential message of that confession—and all the rest—is not the six days. Rather, it is that God is Creator and that creation is very good.

In other generations, in both the Presbyterian Church (U.S.A.) and in the Presbyterian Church U.S., some who believed as I were tried for heresy. Now, however, it seems that Presbyterians want to heal those divisions and allow differences in belief about creation in light of varying backgrounds and interests. The *Book of Order*, for example, says simply that "God created the heavens and the earth and made human beings in God's image, charging them to care for all that lives" (G-3.0101a).

Most important, God the Creator did not "wind up the world" like a clock at the beginning of its existence and then just let it go. Presbyterians have consistently linked the creation of the universe with words about God's providential care for it. From the *Book of Order* comes the statement about the "providence of God who creates, sustains, rules, and redeems the world"(G-2.0500a). Every time Presbyterians speak of creation, we naturally follow with a word about providence.

### God Cares for All

Jesus, to show the care of God, pointed to some common things: "Look at the birds of the air; they neither sow nor reap nor gather into barns, and yet your heavenly Father feeds them. . . . Consider the lilies of the field. . . . But if God so clothes the grass of the field, . . . will he not much more clothe you?" (Matt. 6:26–30). Frequently Jesus and his disciples depended on God's loving care. The general affirmation of God's loving care is called "providence."

Providence speaks of God's care for creation. Therefore, said Calvin, Christian faith has no room for fortune or fate. Fortune, the belief that chance sometimes rules in the world, we express with such statements as "That's the way the cookie crumbles." Fate, a crueler belief, considers that everyone loses in the end. If fortune is the rolling of some cosmic dice, fate is the rolling of dice always loaded against us. Both fate and fortune indicate a realm of life independent of the rule of God. Reformed faith, at its core, says there is no realm of life outside God's protection and love. Sometimes I tease Presbyterian friends by saying, "As one Calvinist to another, I wish you good luck!" I am teasing because Reformed faith teaches God's care, not "luck." So-called natural occurrences continue to receive attention from God. Human direction in life comes from God's calling each person into the future.

Reformed faith declares God's providence both from the overwhelming witness of Scripture and from the simplest argument of logic. Both Bible and reason cry "Providence." Abraham, Moses, Deborah, Saul, David, exiled Israelites, Nehemiah, Elizabeth, Mary, Peter, Paul, Cornelius, Lois, Eunice, and Timothy all testify to God's work in their lives, according to the Bible. These are just a few of the characters in whom the work of God can be seen.

By the same token, the very definition of God in classical terms means that God is all-knowing, all-powerful, and everywhere (omniscient, omnipotent, and omnipresent). If God is all-knowing and all-powerful, then it follows that God's knowledge of something is the same as its occurrence. All this is true just from the definitions of the words, although it can be seen in fact.

Reformed faith, however, has quickly spoken of the mystery in this process. Human beings do not know, nor can we claim to manipulate, the secret and majestic providence of God. Why did

God choose the people of Israel as bearers of a special covenant? Why did God choose to send Jesus Christ as redeemer and the Holy Spirit as sustainer and comforter? We do not know how God's providence works, except as God reveals the loving and just outcomes of it through Scripture and the ongoing creation. We do know that God's providence continues, and at times our certainty of that fact is more important than our questions or doubts. That certainty is not perfect either, as nothing is perfect among human beings. Rather, it is the certainty of faith, especially in times of great need for solace.

## God Cares for You and Me

The miracle in trusting God's providence is that we know it personally. We can see God's care in our lives. For me, it is mostly by looking back over my shoulder in time, so to speak, that I can clearly see God's guidance and control. I imagine the same is true with all Christians, who can understand and view God's grace at work in events and relationships that did not at first seem to be providential at all. In losing a loved one especially, people have later confirmed that God was at work. Faith is God's gift.

Elsie Robinson, who knew in that congregational event that God's "got the whole world in his hands," received her faith as a gift. It is by faith alone, by grace alone, and by Scripture alone that she can believe in God's creation and God's providence.

## Chapter Three

# To Follow Jesus

Our pastor at Highland Presbyterian Church in Louisville in the 1980s, Jim Chatham, did not shy from difficult subjects. Particularly concerning race and civil rights in America, Jim followed biblical texts to speak of justice and mercy. One Sunday, preaching on Jeremiah, he used the illustration of Albert, a man he had known from a previous pastorate in Mississippi. A car dealer and a Christian in the 1960s, he spoke out as a white for justice for black people. He stood courageously for civil rights at the cost of local patronage and popularity. Jim told of how the Ku Klux Klan had burned a cross in Albert's yard and destroyed a number of his cars on the sales lot. Jim said that when he heard the simple testimony of this Christian, he sensed he was standing on "holy ground."

The next week, a member of Highland reported that, having been convicted by Jim's sermon, he had resigned from a prestigious country club in town that prohibited African Americans from joining. That episode occurred before we attended Highland, but several times we heard Jim tell about Christian witness and following Jesus. Before the "WWJD" bracelets became so popular, we heard Jim asking, "What would Jesus do?" concerning numbers of situations in town and more broadly in the world.

## On All Sides of Issues

When Carolyn and I belonged at Anchorage, one evening our phone rang. "Hello, this is Mary Bell," said the voice on the other end. Mary, a longtime member of the church, asked for help. "They are having a hearing on scattered-site housing next week, and one of the proposed locations is not far from the church. We ought to support this scattered-site proposal if it seems to be good for the poor," she said. "Will you take it to the Care and Outreach Committee? I'll be out of town tomorrow night. Herb and I will be back and able to go to the hearing next week."

Reformed Christians have understood that Christianity is both a belief system and a way of life. To follow Jesus does not mean that we will necessarily favor scattered-site housing in our neighborhood. In fact we had major disagreements on that issue. When I went to the hearing, members of the congregation spoke on several sides concerning scattered-site housing. But Presbyterians since the beginning of our tradition have struggled to make actions and faith consonant with one another.

I find that sometimes I try harder to follow Jesus than at other times. Mary Bell said she did too. I suspect that all Presbyterians have more capable and less capable times, that some folks are more disciplined in seeking to follow Jesus than others. Moreover, times change. To follow Jesus has meant different things for Presbyterians in different ages. Today we try also. What guidance do we have as we seek to follow Jesus? We look at the mystery of the nature of Jesus himself, at the work of Jesus for us, and at the process of appropriating trust in God.

## The Ministry of Jesus

As Jesus began his ministry, he called to Peter and Andrew, to James and John, and to others, "Come, follow me." Jesus then went about doing good, and he instructed his disciples to "go and do likewise." He told his followers many things that would help as they attempted to follow him. The act of following Jesus makes the Christian just as much as believing certain things about Jesus, God, and the Spirit.

Jesus healed people, for example. He sought their welfare. When friends lowered a paralyzed man through the roof, Jesus healed the man and told him that his sins had been forgiven because his friends had faith (Luke 5:18–24). Jesus healed a woman with a hemorrhage, the daughter of Jairus, a leper, a crazed man, and many others. When a Syrophoenician woman asked Jesus to heal her daughter, he did it and showed that his caring crossed ethnic and racial boundaries (Mark 7:24–30). He cared for everyone, and he sought the welfare of all.

Jesus paid attention to ordinary, human needs—especially the needs of the poor. When crowds came to hear him and to be healed, people became so enthralled with him that they did not leave to eat: "Then Jesus called his disciples to him and said, 'I have compassion for the crowd, because they have been with me now for three days and have nothing to eat'" (Matt. 15:32). He produced food for their needs. When a rich young man asked Jesus what he must do to receive eternal life, Jesus told him first to obey the law. Then Jesus, who loved the man, said, "Go, sell what you own, and give the money to the poor, and you will have treasure in heaven; then come, follow me" (Mark 10:21).

Jesus also showed his disciples what they should do in order to follow him. They should become trusting, as little children are. They should also heal people where possible. They should give generously to the poor. They should care for the outcasts. At one point, Jesus even said that in caring for the needy, followers would be caring for Jesus himself: "Then the righteous will answer him, 'Lord, when was it that we saw you hungry and gave you food, or thirsty and gave you something to drink? And when was it that we saw you a stranger and welcomed you, or naked and gave you clothing?' And the king will answer them, 'Truly I tell you, as you did it to one of the least of these who are members of my family, you did it to me'" (Matt. 25:37–40).

In his ministry Jesus fulfilled the law of God. Matthew's Gospel particularly keeps pointing out that Jesus healed and taught "in order to fulfill what was spoken through the prophet" (Matt.

8:17; 12:17). His interpretation of the law differed from that generally understood in his day. He even healed on the Sabbath, in violation of the rigid laws. In his actions, Jesus showed that God expected obedience in acts of justice and mercy, not in merely doing the prescribed ritual acts of religion. The ministry of Jesus was an all-encompassing life of service and compassion, done in obedience to God's purpose for people.

Presbyterians, as other Christians, consider that in his death Jesus also ministered by fulfilling the law in accord with God's providence. Jesus prayed, "Father, if you are willing, remove this cup from me; yet, not my will but yours be done" (Luke 22:42). When he was crucified, Jesus "became obedient to the point of death—even death on a cross" (Phil. 2:8). The centurion in charge of the execution and all the rest of the people could see in the earthquake and darkness that accompanied the death of Jesus that "truly, this was God's Son" (Matt. 27:54).

Jesus, perfectly obedient in life and death, did what no other human being had been able to do. Paul and other early Christian preachers showed the contrast between the life of Jesus and the lives of others such as Abraham and David (Rom. 4). Most of all, they contrasted the disobedience of Adam (and Eve) with the obedience of Jesus Christ. From the very first existence of human beings, sin had been a portion of human experience. Now in Christ Jesus, through faith, people could be freed from the dominion of sin. The ministry of Jesus included dying "for the ungodly." He overcame death's power for believers:

> Therefore, just as sin came into the world through one man, and death came through sin, and so death spread to all because all have sinned—sin was indeed in the world before the law, but sin is not reckoned when there is no law. Yet death exercised dominion from Adam to Moses, even over those whose sins were not like the transgression of Adam, who is a type of the one who was to come. (Rom. 5:12–14)

Reformed leaders saw Christ's ministry as the beginning of a new eon in history. They followed a Christian tradition that spoke of the time after Jesus Christ as a "covenant of grace." Later sections of this introduction will take up some of the particular parts of this "covenant theology," as it came to be called. Suffice it to say at this point that it has been important for several strains of Presbyterians. Many think it still is the most accurate way to speak of the ministry of Christ. He ushered in the covenant of grace.

In his own ministry, Jesus told followers how to live. He did not just show them. He said that the traditional law of religious people did not go far enough in demanding righteousness. "You have heard it said, . . . 'You shall not murder.' . . . But I say to you that if you are angry with a brother or sister, you will be liable to judgment" (Matt. 5:21–22). Jesus reinterpreted others of the Ten Commandments and of the laws, so that people could see God demanded wholehearted obedience in mind and spirit as well as in deed.

When that rich young man came to Jesus, he was told first to obey the regular law. Then Jesus called for further obedience. When Jesus taught about justice, he called for believers to go beyond merely paying back debts or doing their duty. "You have heard that it was said, 'An eye for an eye and a tooth for a tooth.' But I also say to you, Do not resist an evildoer. But if anyone strikes you on the right cheek, turn the other also" (Matt. 5:38–39). Go the extra mile. Pray for those who persecute you. On and on the commands of Christ called for followers to be more like Jesus himself.

## The Atonement

Even though Jim Chatham, Albert, Mary Bell, and all the rest of us are trying to follow Jesus, we realize that we cannot perfectly obey the law of God. Only through the life and death of Jesus Christ have we participated in full obedience. Though some Christian traditions today emphasize only the example of Jesus in living, most, including the Presbyterian tradition, still consider the death of Jesus as a center of that ministry for us.

Just how we are reconciled to God through the work of Jesus Christ has been the subject of great debate. All the various images or theories both of the ways Jesus worked to reconcile and of the atonement came from the Bible. Was Jesus the moral example, living and dying so that others might see how to live and die? Was Jesus the payment by God of a kind of ransom to the powers of sin and death, so that believers could be freed from those powers? Was Jesus the cosmic victor over the evil one, whose armies had controlled the world since the beginning of history, subject only to the overarching powers of God? Was Jesus the substitution of a guiltless victim for the guilty ones (people) to satisfy God's own justice? Again, all of these theories had bases in Scripture. Reformed theologians have not usually denied the truth of any of them.

Reformed Christians, however, have generally depended on the image of Jesus Christ, the substitute for human beings, in considering the nature of the atonement. In Calvin's *Institutes*, the question is asked, "What . . . would Christ have bestowed upon us if the penalty for our sins were still required?" The answer, following 1 Peter 2:24 and other portions of Scripture, is "Lo, you see plainly that Christ bore the penalty of sins to deliver his own people from them" (*Institutes* 3.4.30). In the feisty words of the Scots Confession, "[We believe] that our Lord Jesus offered himself a voluntary sacrifice unto his Father for us, that he suffered contradiction of sinners, that he was wounded and plagued for our transgressions, that he, the clean innocent Lamb of God, was condemned in the presence of an earthly judge, that we should be absolved before the judgment seat of our God" (Scots Confession 3.09).

## Human Sin

The ministry of Christ and his atonement show just how much we need both. Presbyterians historically have paid a great deal of attention to the Bible's teachings that "all have sinned and fall short of the glory of God" (Rom. 3:23). The doctrine has been called "total depravity." By this, Presbyterians and other Calvinists have meant that every part of the human being is affected by sin. Every act continues tinged by sin. No person or action can be entirely free from sin. Only Jesus Christ lived, died, and rose as an exception to this universal sinfulness.

Presbyterians in former centuries took some pleasure in this doctrine of total depravity, it must be admitted. However, more recently the various Presbyterian churches have modified the most blatant statements of it, along with some of the other "harsh" words of traditional Calvinism. But still nothing done in this world is perfect, according to Presbyterian confessions.

Take the sin of segregation, which plagued the whole nation and still presents occasion for many white people to avoid including people of color. All of us are to some degree complicit in it—if only that whites, African Americans, and others avoid difficult conversations and allow racially charged jokes to pass unanswered by rejection. Or take the example of scattered-site housing, which has presented itself in many of our communities. Every action, including doing nothing about providing adequate housing for the poor, contains inevitable sin. Even a creative and viable solution to a human situation calls forth self-righteousness or some other proud feeling. The self-interest of builders, speculators, bureaucrats, church people, and many others is involved in the situation. In brief, those who favor the proposal, those who oppose it, and those who want to take no action will all be involved in human sin. So will our communities, our social systems, and our churches that own property. That is the condition of human depravity, which confessions say has existed since the very first human beings lived.

As the study moves along, we shall return to the subject of human sin. Right now it is important to see it as a belief that is related to our attempts to follow Jesus. It helps us understand the Reformed teachings about God's work to bring us into the communion of saints. It helps put in perspective what we mean when we promise to follow Jesus and depend on him alone. That process of salvation, in traditional words "the economy of redemption," also pertains to the following of Jesus.

### Effectual Calling

Presbyterians spent considerable energy working out a vocabulary to describe the process of appropriation of atonement. "Effectual calling" was just one of the terms. Others have included "justification," "repentance," "adoption," and "sanctification." It is significant that all these words came originally from the Bible, and they represent a logical progression as well. The process began as and remains God's gift, and human beings could do nothing outside of God's gifts to start it or to speed it along. These are traditional terms used to describe the process in which we have become followers of Jesus, realizing that we cannot do what Jesus did.

Effectual calling means that God does the work in permitting us to believe and to try following Jesus. In the words of the Westminster Shorter Catechism, "Effectual calling is the work of God's Spirit, whereby, convincing us of our sin and misery, enlightening our minds in the knowledge of Christ, and renewing our wills, he doth persuade and enable us to embrace Jesus Christ, freely offered to us in the gospel" (A.31). In the words of Paul, it is the "spirit of wisdom and of revelation" that enlightens "the eyes of your hearts" so "you may know what is the hope to which he has called you" (Eph. 1:18).

In the sequence of trying to follow Jesus, we are first enabled to repent, to recognize the sinfulness in which we exist and call upon God for forgiveness. We are then permitted to sense that God does not count our sin against us, because Christ intercedes for us. Then we experience the falling away of sin and the restoring of our relationship as children of God. Finally, we begin the process of following Jesus.

## Chapter Four

# To Live in the Spirit

When Dick Hays approached me at coffee time, I could tell he had a question on his mind. "Before we go upstairs to worship, can you tell me about the charismatics?"

"Well, Dick," I responded, "what do you want to know?"

"We were reading Acts in Sunday school. What happened when the Spirit came? Are we Presbyterians just as able to have gifts of the Spirit as those early church folk? And do the charismatics have them?"

Dick Hays always asked good questions, usually much deeper than a coffee-break response can plumb. Today, questions about the nature and teachings of the Holy Spirit come from longtime Presbyterians such as he. They come even more quickly from Christians who have been members of Holiness or Pentecostal churches and now belong to a Presbyterian body.

There are many ways to speak about the work of the Holy Spirit. Reformed leaders have considered the Bible telling about the Spirit as "proceeding from the Father and the Son," as the Western part of the church declared centuries ago. The Holy Spirit is the agent of holiness (or sanctification), the giver of authority, and the power of God for reconciliation, according to church doctrine. The gifts of the Spirit are important to mention also.

### Proceeding from the Father and Son

The Gospels are full of references to the Spirit as coming from God. In the accounts of the birth of Jesus Christ, for example, the statements about Mary's conception refer to the Holy Spirit (Matt. 1:18; Luke 1:35). In the accounts of Jesus being baptized by John, the Spirit of God descended "like a dove." The voice from heaven said, "This is my Son, the Beloved, with whom I am well pleased" (Matt. 3:16). When Jesus sent out disciples for the first time, he told them not to worry. "The Spirit of [their] Father" would speak through them (Matt. 10:20). Words from the prophets fulfilled by actions of Jesus included those from Isaiah about the servant with God's Spirit "upon him" (Matt. 12:18).

Again, almost as many passages speak of the Spirit coming from Jesus Christ himself. Jesus was perceived as "full of the Holy Spirit" (Luke 4:1). After his resurrection, Jesus appeared to his disciples and said, "Peace be with you." Then he breathed on them and said, "Receive the Holy Spirit" (John 20:22). He promised that his Spirit, the Comforter, would be with disciples, and early leaders considered the Spirit as being from Jesus Christ as well as from God the Father.

It seems that through much of Christian history, people did not work as hard on developing the doctrines about Christ. For the most part, they simply confirmed the standard creeds. The creed from Constantinople (AD 381) had said that the church believed in the "Holy Spirit, the Lord and Giver of life, . . . who is worshiped and glorified together with the Father and the Son, who spoke through the prophets."

Even this much doctrine caused splits among Christians (as we saw about the Trinity in chapter 2). Some said the Spirit could not proceed from the Son as from the Father. For most Christians it has been simple to think of God as transcendent Creator on the one hand, and as incarnate Redeemer on the other. This third person of the Trinity could not be put in a logical place, although most Protestants have kept a doctrine of the Spirit somewhere in their minds. Both Disciples of Christ and Presbyterians at certain times have tended to downplay the divinity of the Holy Spirit as a distinct entity within the Godhead.

In the early years of the twentieth century, both the Presbyterian Church (U.S.A.) and the Presbyterian Church U.S. amended the Westminster Confession of Faith in order to include chapters on the Holy Spirit.

In revising the creed, Presbyterians emphasized that the Spirit proceeds from the Father and the Son. They said also, with the early church leaders, that the Holy Spirit should receive faith, love, obedience, and praise with the other persons of Trinity. However, contemporary Presbyterians also emphasize that the Holy Spirit is active in the work of redemption. They likewise tell of the work of the Spirit in uniting believers in the church universal.

## Agent of Holiness

In the work of redemption, the Holy Spirit is the grace of God calling people from sinful, self-centered lives, into worship and praise of God. Paul spoke of the Spirit ushering in God's new relationship with people:

> For the law of the Spirit of life in Christ Jesus has set you free from the law of sin and death. . . . For those who live according to the flesh set their minds upon the things of the flesh, but those who live according to the Spirit set their minds on the things of the Spirit. To set the mind on the flesh is death, but to set the mind on the Spirit is life and peace. (Rom. 8:2, 5–6)

Through the Spirit come regeneration, repentance, adoption, and freedom in Christ. Through the Spirit comes the will to "be perfect, as your heavenly Father is perfect" (Matt. 5:48). Through the Spirit comes even prayer itself, intercession with God in behalf of ourselves and others.

Reformed Christians have understood about growth in Christ and the seeking of perfection. We have believed that holiness grows in discipleship, the process of sanctification. In the words of John Calvin, "The closer a [person] comes to the likeness of God, the more the image of God shines in him" (*Institutes* 3.3.8)

If sin persists in the lives of believers, how does the Spirit yield freedom, holiness, and prayer? Presbyterians have affirmed that God makes believers better than they had been. Just because we cannot in this life be perfect does not excuse us from doing our best to follow Jesus, to live in the Spirit. What is begun in this life God completes for the faithful. We pay close attention to the examples of Simon Peter, the apostle Paul, and others in that early church. None of them became perfect, we say, although a number were heroic Christians.

Paul wrote almost constantly of the work of the Spirit in his own process of "putting on Christ," his process of sanctification. Yet Paul realized that he continued to sin. It was in that context that he told early Christians they were being "sanctified by the Holy Spirit" (Rom. 15:16).

Both Catholics and members of the Holiness wing of the Methodist movement have different views about the sanctifying work of the Holy Spirit. The Catholic Church has traditionally taught that God gives special gifts to some Christians through the Spirit. When believers cooperate with those gifts, more merit is created than necessary for the salvation of that particular believer. The extra merit becomes available for other Christians who need it. All the good comes from God, but with the special saints sharing, they intercede for us. This very complex doctrine, developed over centuries of theology, contrasts somewhat with Presbyterian reliance on God's Spirit (grace) alone. Both points of view have basis in Scripture, and today we see more in common than not about the Spirit's agency in behalf of sanctification.

The Holiness wing in Methodism, which developed through the nineteenth century among different Protestant denominations, teaches that any believer can be perfect in this life. While the United Methodist Church and other mainstream denominations would not make such bold statements, the founder of Methodism, John Wesley, did say Christians needed to hear Christ's command: "Be perfect." Wesley and the Methodist tradition doubtless helped Presbyterians in the eighteenth century and, more recently, opened up discussion of the nature of the Holy Spirit. But Holiness communions accused Catholics, Presbyterians, and regular Methodists of being lazy and only half trusting the power of the Spirit to make people perfect.

Presbyterians, in dialogue with other bodies in reforming our own thought, have grown to say more about the Spirit in recent decades. Some Presbyterians might even believe that people can be perfect in this life, but a vast majority of us believe that life in the Spirit does not rule out the fact that we continue to sin within this life. We see God empowering us to grow in faith, to make more mature decisions, and to love more faithfully. We see the Holy Spirit providing Christian freedom in which we can live, but we do not view ourselves as perfect. Personally, I take solace and energy from this belief. I fully expect other Presbyterians, including Dick Hays, do too.

### Giver of Authority

Presbyterians also believe that the Holy Spirit provides authority for the believer. The Spirit, for example, enabled the writers of Scripture to speak truthfully about God, Jesus Christ, and all the rest of the things necessary for us to know. We say the Bible writers were in-*spired* by the *Spirit*. We believe that the same Spirit enables us to read and interpret the Bible for ourselves in community. In the famous words of John Calvin, it is the "inward witness of the Holy Spirit" that seals biblical authority for us.

Though a few may have sounded like they believed it, no Presbyterians I know have ever argued that the Bible by magic could answer all things with full certainty for the believer. On the other hand, no Presbyterian I know has said the Bible is "just another book." Presbyterians want to stress that God's Spirit gives the Bible its power to help and to teach us. The church does not give the Bible power; rather the Bible, as interpreted through the Spirit, gives the church power.

As the Spirit gives authority in the writing and reading of Scripture, so it also gives authority to the church. Presbyterians believe that church councils, confessions, and assemblies can err. But they still have more authority than does the isolated Christian. Though God alone is Lord of the conscience, Christians are to realize the power of the Spirit working within the life of the church. Such a realization brings modesty. The Christian can be made "teachable," ready to grow in grace, with humility and a willingness to listen to the true church.

In fact, the Holy Spirit gives authority to all powers recognized on earth for good. In the words of the Westminster Confession of Faith as amended in the twentieth century:

> By the indwelling of the Holy Spirit all believers being vitally united to Christ, who is the head, are thus united one to another in the Church, which is his body. He calls and anoints ministers for their holy office, qualifies all other officers in the Church for their special work, and imparts various gifts and graces to its members. He gives efficacy to the Word and to the ordinances of the gospel. By him the Church will be preserved, increased, purified, and at last made perfectly holy in the presence of God. (6.186)

This statement ties together nicely the Reformed understanding of the Holy Spirit's providing authority with the corporate nature of the church. It also affirms that the Holy Spirit gives various gifts, a response to the question from Dick Hays.

### Giver of Gifts

The apostle Paul spoke eloquently about the gifts of the Spirit:

> To one is given through the Spirit the utterance of wisdom, to another the utterance of knowledge according to the same Spirit, to another faith by the same Spirit, to another gifts of healing by the one Spirit, to another the working of miracles, to another prophecy, to another the discernment of spirits, to another various kinds of tongues, to another the interpretation of tongues. (1 Cor. 12:8–10)

Each of the gifts has been given for the common good, as each part of the body helps make the whole.

At several points Paul made lists of what he called "the fruit of the Spirit." In one place he said, "The fruit of the Spirit is love, joy, peace, patience, kindness, generosity, faithfulness, gentleness, and self-control" (Gal. 5:22). Presbyterians have seen all these as gifts of the Holy Spirit. The Holy Spirit also gives each person a sense of "calling" to a special function in the world, in keeping with God's providence and Christ's summons to follow him. In these ways, Presbyterians have consistently been "charismatics." We have been consciously dependent on the charismata from God—God's Spirit's gifts.

In recent years, as at several previous times in Christian history, speaking in tongues has become important for many Christians. This phenomenon occurred during the great revivals of the early nineteenth century, for example, along with other physical symptoms of religious experience. Presbyterians in those days generally discouraged believers from speaking in tongues and from other "spiritual exercises," as they called them. In the twentieth-century movement, Presbyterians reacted in a more positive manner. Now several thousands of Presbyterians who speak in tongues feel that they have an important place in the church. Presbyterians who speak in tongues consider that the Holy Spirit gives the gift, as other gifts. In some congregations, factions have arisen between those speaking in tongues and those with other commitments. In other congregations, however, different groups have found mutual goals and worship together.

A Presbyterian may speak in tongues, but certainly none has to. By the same token, a Presbyterian may feel uncomfortable with fellow worshipers speaking in tongues. Indeed, the same thing may be true for many other aspects of congregational worship and life. As long as the other gifts of the Spirit are present—utterance of wisdom, utterance of knowledge, faith, and the like—Presbyterians can make good accounting of the gifts of tongues and interpretations of tongues. And the most important thing is the fruit of the Spirit—love, joy, peace, patience, and all the rest.

## Chapter Five

# To Walk in the Way

Sunday morning. Second service. The pastor at Williamsburg Presbyterian, Patrick Willson, stands in the pulpit to
read the story of the Sending of the Seventy from the Gospel
of Luke:

> Go on your way. See, I am sending you out like lambs into
> the midst of wolves. Carry no purse, no bag, no sandals; and
> greet no one on the road. . . . Whenever you enter a town
> and its people welcome you, eat what is set before you, cure
> the sick who are there, and say to them, "The kingdom of
> God has come near to you." (10:3–9)

Already we have heard a minute for mission, some of the con-
cerns of the church, and a call to worship. We have sung the
hymn "God Is Here," as the choir processed. We have prayed
prayers of adoration and confession together, and we have heard
an assurance of pardon. We have sung a Gloria Patri, listened to
a reading from Isaiah, and read Psalm 40 responsively.

Patrick is beginning a series on "The Great Ends of the
Church," and today he preaches on "the proclamation of the gospel for the salvation of humankind." He explains that the message
of salvation is Jesus' message, that its power comes from the Holy
Spirit and not from us:

Jesus sends his followers out to bless: "Whatever house you enter, first say, 'Peace to this house!'" "Peace"—shalom— is a one-word summary of all the good God wants to give us. Far from simply being the absence of war or an interval between conflict, peace—shalom—invokes everything God intends for human creatures: life, joy, land, fertility, health, children, long life, wealth, laughter.

Following the sermon, we welcome new members into the congregation. Ushers take the offering, and we pass the peace and sing a closing hymn. After the benediction, we assemble in the fellowship hall for coffee.

The sermon, the Scripture lessons, the singing, the welcoming of new members, and the fellowship with one another—the whole worship service together forms a part of our "walking in the way" of the Christian faith as Presbyterians. We consider that the worship, the sacraments, the singing, the proclamation of the Word of God, and the gathering of the congregation are all important for us. Distinctive for Presbyterians is the preaching and hearing of the Word as a "mark of the church," a necessary part of our being disciples. But the whole experience fits in one piece with the life we lead as a portion of our obedience.

The early Christians at times called their new life "the Way." They followed the Scriptures, by which they meant the books of the Old Testament. These, together with the changes and the new instruction of the Way (writings that have become for us the New Testament) led the Christians in discipleship. We have already looked briefly at the authority of Scripture, but let us note now the authority of the Reformed tradition and the leadership of the church for teaching us "the Way" of discipleship.

### The Presbyterian Way

Gradually, one wing of Protestants in the sixteenth century came to practice representative government. Members of this Reformed wing, with their special emphases in theology already mentioned and special beliefs about sacraments and the nature of law yet to be discussed, also agreed that certain forms of church government followed Scripture. They saw themselves as heirs to the biblical patterns of government, and they saw these patterns as helpful for those seeking to be disciples in their own day.

Presbyterians have considered representative government, the selection of elders especially, as a process faithful to the organization of ancient Israel as well as that of the early church. The Old Testament often spoke of elders, and the Jewish faith communities had elders in the time of Jesus Christ. Presbyterians note the appointment of elders in the first local congregations (Acts 14:23), their selection of Paul and Barnabas, and the role of elders in the council at Jerusalem. Why, the Pastoral Epistles even tell what kind of person should be an elder! A leader should "not be arrogant or quick-tempered or a drunkard or violent or greedy for gain, but hospitable, a lover of goodness, master of himself, upright, holy, and self-controlled" (Titus 1:7–9).

From the Greek word for "elder," *presbyteros*, came the name for Presbyterians, "those ruled by elders." Presbyterian pioneers considered the word "elder" a synonym in the New Testament for the word "bishop," a word of importance for Catholic, Anglican, and Methodist Christians, among others. Presbyterians since the time of John Calvin have considered that some elders need to be trained for proclamation of the Word especially, while others need to be in all kinds of Christian vocations as lay leaders. The teaching elders, or minister, and the ruling elders, or lay leaders, should share power in the church. Though Presbyterian denominations have developed differently in various countries, this accent on shared leadership has remained remarkably consistent.

Leaders chosen from the local congregation as ruling elders, together with a teaching elder, or minister of Word and Sacrament, govern the local, or "particular," church. Elders of both kinds form a presbytery, a court governing the life of congregations in a local area. Representatives from various presbyteries comprise a synod, a regional court. And representatives from all the presbyteries in a denomination gather for the General Assembly.

As congregations and church courts have become more complex in our own country, other people have been selected by various courts to be responsible for particular programs or meeting certain needs—in missions, for example, or in evangelism. In addition, as local churches have grown, many have called more than one minister to serve them. The size and complexity of Presbyterianism has demanded the adoption of many rules for congregations, church courts, ministers, and leaders. The *Book of Order* in large measure spells out the "Presbyterian Way" of representative government in our denomination.

We Presbyterians do not have to believe in this Presbyterian Way in the same way we believe in God. In fact, wise Presbyterians through the centuries have recognized that other Christians can be just as faithful by following different forms of government, whether congregational or episcopal. I have found representative church government frustrating at times, but I have grown to love the way in which God's Spirit seems to permit courts to rise above differences in beliefs and opinions to unite in integrated work and worship.

We Presbyterians believe church courts are not perfect, just as we believe Christians are not perfect in this life. But we understand that representative courts can sometimes check the errors of individuals. As the whole church of God is a community—one body of Christ—so the representatives of the larger church usually embody the wisdom of Christ better than do solitary believers. When selected as representatives to church courts, we should serve with care and diligence. When our presbytery speaks, or our General Assembly, we should listen. And we realize that the *Book of Order* can be changed in accord with the wills of General Assemblies (with presbyteries concurring).

Some decades ago, for example, Presbyterian leaders in all the major denominations in the United States came to see that women should share in the formal government of the church and in the proclamation of the Word. Interestingly, this insight came for Presbyterians about the same time as for Methodists, a little later than to the Congregational Church, and a little before the Lutherans and Episcopalians. Gradually, editions of the *Book of Order* were changed first to permit women to organize their own areas of leadership and work in local churches, then to permit women to address church bodies, then to permit the ordination of women as teaching and ruling elders, and now to urge church courts fairly to select women in accord with female membership in the church. It seemed to me that the various changes took place far too slowly. But I know others in the church who think the changes occurred much too rapidly. Yet we all remain committed to the representative form of government, which moves in organic fashion to respond to God's will in changing situations (more about this subject in chapter 13).

We Presbyterians follow the Presbyterian Way in our attempts to be faithful disciples of Jesus Christ. In following Jesus, we really become disciples to the Master.

## Discipleship

Life in the early church was filled with worship, service, and education. Notice how much the early church remembered worship and the power of the sermons in worship. Peter preached at Pentecost, when the Holy Spirit gave power to the disciples. In the course of worship and fasting, the Christian elders in Antioch made their decision to send Paul and Barnabas as missionaries (Acts 13:2). Eutychus even fell from the upper window when he slept during worship, and he received healing from the apostles (Acts 20:9).

One of the elements in discipleship involves a commitment to attend worship. Presbyterians do not have rules about attending worship. If people fail to show any commitment, then the leaders of a Presbyterian congregation have a responsibility to put their names on an inactive role. But no one has to go to worship. On the other hand, the center of worship is praise of God and instruction in the Way. What better way is a Presbyterian led in learning about God and about the faith than in worship?

Perhaps more significant than merely being there in worship is the active listening and participation expected of members in Presbyterian churches. Discipleship involves keeping one's ears open, especially to the reading of Scripture, to the proclamation of the Word, and to the celebration of the sacraments. I guess it is more properly put to "keep one's heart and mind open." In the sermon Patrick Willson preached, we listeners could learn a great deal about the nature of God, about the transmission of the faith, and about our own responsibilities. Those teachings seem to me implicit in Scripture itself, but Patrick brought them out for us to hear and understand.

There are patterns of Presbyterian worship, based in part on the Western liturgy of the Roman Catholic Church, from which we have come. Also a part of our tradition is the reading of Scripture in the language of the people, the preaching of a sermon that explains the Scripture and applies it for our lives, and the singing of hymns of praise. We also engage in public prayer, with words formed for us by the minister and other worship leaders. Patterns of worship change, but they remain rather consistent at the same time. These patterns are described in the Directory for Worship that, like the *Book of Order*, possesses authority for us. It describes the ways in which Anchorage Presbyterian Church and all other congregations should render worship. Our pastors and any associate pastors, the session, and all the rest of us use the Directory for Worship as a guide for our corporate worship.

Discipleship involves worship—and a great deal more. For Reformed Christians, service in worship is preparation for service in the world. Our discipleship involves proclaiming the gospel as well as we can in whatever we do. That is a full-time job! Being a member of the Way means that we listen to Jesus' words:

> You are the light of the world. A city built on a hill cannot be hid. No one after lighting a lamp puts it under a bushel basket, but on the lampstand, and it gives light to all in the house. In the same way, let your light so shine before others, so that they may see your good works and give glory to your Father in heaven. (Matt. 5:14–16)

Discipleship then means that we Presbyterians are to let our light shine. Sometimes it means telling others that we believe in Jesus Christ and inviting them to do the same. Sometimes it means that we invite others to join us in worship. Sometimes it means that we actually go to other communities and other lands to serve

Jesus Christ by helping people there learn about God. Sometimes it means that we have to take an unpopular stand at work, school, or in social groups. Sometimes it means that we help people simply because they need help—they are hungry, thirsty, in prison, or strangers.

Discipleship has all kinds of meaning for us. How can we know what should be done or said? In many cases we look to the Bible for instruction. We also look to the tradition of the church, not just to follow what has been done before but also to learn in our own day what it means to be obedient. We follow the leading of those who have preceded us. We look to the leaders of the Presbyterian Church, speaking through General Assemblies and other courts. All the while we realize that our discipleship will not be perfect. God saves us by grace, through faith—not by judging the life we lead. Still, we try to let our light shine so people seeing us will give God the glory.

### Discipline

Presbyterians have a special tradition of exercising church discipline. In earlier times—on the American frontier, for example—church courts dealt with matters of social concern and commerce. I enjoy telling about the minutes of one presbytery in which a minister was brought to trial for selling a horse to an elder. The minister alleged that the horse was healthy, but the animal died a few days later. More serious were church court cases dealing with abuse of slaves, with immorality among elders, and with people engaging in "unhealthy work." Sometimes the cases seemed unfair, such as the one in South Carolina where a telephone operator was disciplined for working on Sunday. Often, though, the cases helped Presbyterians understand in real terms that being a disciple involved discipline. "The purpose of discipline is to honor God by making clear the significance of membership in the body of Christ," reads the Principles of Church Discipline (D-1.0101), which is published as part of the *Book of Order*.

Church discipline among Presbyterians follows the Rules of Discipline. These rules look like those of any formal body. They exist to permit structures for dissent, to specify jurisdiction, and to regulate discipline of members and courts of the church. Almost all the time, however, church discipline merely stands as a possibility for redress as the church goes about its business. After all, the business of the church (as the business of believers) is love of God and neighbors. In the Presbyterian Church, love of neighbor remains exceedingly important.

*Chapter Six*

# To Love Your Neighbor

I s there room for me too?" Jean Elliot asked as she hopped on the bus in Anchorage. Louis Coleman, director of the Presbyterian Community Center, began explaining to us about the center's functions as we rode together to see it. Our Sunday school class, with Mrs. Elliot and several other interested members of the wider congregation, took a Sunday afternoon to learn about the needs at the center and about some things we could do to help. The Rademaker family, the Gillises, the Milwoods, the Cunninghams, the Perkeys, the Troys, Bob Hawkes, and several more of us ate lunch together, boarded the school bus, and toured the center.

"This child-care center is the jewel of our program now," Louis Coleman explained as he showed us around. He then introduced us to Mrs. Davis, who directed that program. "With the drying up of government money, the church's contribution will be more crucial," Mrs. Davis told us. She said many families simply leave their young children with unskilled and uninterested residents in the nearby public housing project. "We really need support to enable families to bring their young children here," Rev. Coleman explained.

As we met afterward, our class decided to help support children at the Presbyterian Community Center as a special project in addition to the gifts we give through presbytery for the center. "We ought to be able to give an offering a week for this," Bruce

43

Rademaker declared. We nodded. We reached into our pockets. We told other class members, and they contributed too. It turned into gifts much more than the minimum he suggested.

Anchorage Presbyterian Church was not too big, but we managed to support lots of causes with our time, skill, and money. Members led a "Studio for the Handicapped" program that provided well-constructed materials for the public school children who could not read regular texts, cassettes of articles and books not available elsewhere for the visually handicapped, and an FM station with special programming. Some members were especially interested in an interdenominational mission that houses street people, others in a Salvation Army project, and still others in a college in eastern Kentucky for young people from the mountain area. Some members drove vans to deliver meals to shut-ins. A number of women helped female inmates in a prison ministry. At least two of the members of Anchorage served in a Youth Advocates program, which sought to meet special needs of young offenders. One elder regularly spent her vacation working as a nurse in rural Haiti. On and on the list goes of members in our local church caring and helping, in personal ways and in support of worthwhile institutions.

Next door to the church building is Bellewood Presbyterian Home for Children, a presbytery-sponsored place for families to receive help and for children to reside when necessary. Many other Presbyterian churches in the area helped in other ways. And through the presbytery, synod, and General Assembly we are connected in a network of caring that touches almost every portion of the earth.

In the other churches where Carolyn and I have worshiped and worked, the giving of time, talents, and money has been similar. So at Ginter Park in Richmond, we found ourselves spending the night with forty homeless people when it was that congregation's turn to serve, providing worship for them when a snowstorm prevented the pastor from traveling the next morning. At Highland we assisted in the resettlement of refugees from Eastern Europe and Africa. In Williamsburg, we volunteer in a cooperative food pantry and clothes closet in town. We go to fix meals for homeless people at the church in nearby Newport News. Others in the congregation are working more extensively, by driving people for medical appointments, helping them sign up to receive Medicare, and teaching English as a second (or third, or fourth) language. That is nothing peculiar to Presbyterians, but it is an essential part of being a Presbyterian. Individually and together, we Presbyterians try to love our neighbors as Jesus told us to.

## Christian Care

When a lawyer tested Jesus by asking, "Teacher, what must I do to inherit eternal life?" Jesus replied that he should love God with everything, "and your neighbor as yourself." The inquirer responded with another serious question: "Who is my neighbor?"

Jesus responded with a story of compassion and care. He told the lawyer of a traveler, mugged and left half-dead on the road. A priest passed him by, as did a member of the elite class in society, but a Samaritan, a member of a despised class in Palestine at the time, stopped and gave him personal care. He carried the victim to an inn and paid for his lodging. Jesus asked, "Which of these three, do you think, was a neighbor?" (Luke 10:25–37).

Jesus had many things to say about the responsibility of believers to care for the needy. He said the blessed would be separated from the cursed on the basis of their care for the little people in the world. Jesus said he would not forget even the person who gave a cup of cold water. He himself helped people right and left.

Believers were to "go and do likewise," as Jesus said on several occasions. Christians immediately began to care for one another and for others in need. The record of the church may contain many inglorious moments, but it uniformly shows Christians' care for the needy. In the forming of the Presbyterian wing of the church, pioneers took pains to provide care for the poor. Every strain of the Reformed tradition has maintained care for the needy among its priorities.

Presbyterian care is both individual and structural. Do hungry people need food? Presbyterians in many communities participate in local food pantries, metropolitan-wide efforts to meet emergencies, and legislative attempts to improve the system for people to find jobs and food. At the same time, through our denominational and ecumenical channels we supply vital food for hungry people in Africa, Asia, and Latin America. And we assist in the establishment of demonstration farms in poverty areas that show farmers how to improve production. This emphasis on both the simple and the complex typifies Presbyterian caring.

Nevertheless, many Presbyterians differ in the ways they choose to help. Some even contend against legislative support for the poor. A few believe that meeting individual needs in some countries is a contribution to the problem rather than a solution. All Presbyterians do not agree on the proper methods of helping the poor. Yet one cannot be a practicing Presbyterian without caring and trying in some way to love one's neighbor as oneself. That command of Jesus profoundly affects our response to human need.

What is true in the matters of hunger and food also is true in other matters. What about Presbyterian positions on touchy ethical issues such as environmental protection, abortion, and peacemaking? Do Presbyterians have to believe certain ways about these matters, as some other communions demand?

Christian care Presbyterian style does not demand certain points of view on ethical issues. Some Presbyterians support right-to-life organizations, while others support freedom-of-choice alternatives. Some Presbyterians serve in the armed forces, while others take a pacifist stance on war. Some consider the needs of people more important than environmental considerations; others feel protection of the air, water, and resources come first in behalf of future generations.

To explore in depth these issues and Presbyterian styles of ethical action would demand another whole book. Presbyterians grapple seriously with these complex issues, and this prohibits most from taking an absolute position on them. By the same token, we do not believe that all decisions and actions are equally Christian. Our confessions speak of our being able to do "good works," not entirely pure and unselfish but "acceptable" nonetheless. Certain obvious guidelines help us in some responses to neighbors, and assemblies of the church help in addressing others.

## Bible and Caring

In the first chapter, I promised to deal with the relationship of belief and practice: how do beliefs about God, Jesus Christ, the Spirit, and the church affect values and decision making? By now some general principles have become clear. Jesus explained who neighbors are, for example. The Bible clearly indicates, and we Presbyterians believe, that neighbors include all people. Even those who might be considered "enemies" by some group to which we belong are no longer enemies for us as we seek to follow Christ. "Love your enemies," said Jesus Christ. "Pray for those who persecute you" (Matt. 5:44). We may not be able in immature faith to act upon this clear command of Christ. In fact, at times whole Presbyterian churches have failed to follow the precept and the universal meaning of "neighbor." These failures in the past do not mean that God intends us to keep on in disobedience. Do we have faith in God, seek to follow Christ, and trust life in the Spirit? Then we move to more universal caring about our neighbors, more thorough prayer for all people. A friend suggested that our program as Presbyterians might be "to enlarge the OKOP"—our kind of people. The Bible says that process goes on until we include all.

Again, the Bible is extremely clear about some values—justice, for example. Long before the coming of Christ, the people of Israel understood that their just God required them to seek justice themselves. To exercise justice was to honor God: "The LORD of hosts is exalted by justice," said Isaiah, "and the Holy God shows himself holy by righteousness" (Isa. 5:16). Isaiah warned against turning phrases to subvert their value: "Ah, you who call evil good and good evil, who put darkness for light and light for darkness, who put bitter for sweet and sweet for bitter!" (5:20). God would judge them. The justice in most cases is plain, as Jeremiah, Ezekiel, Micah, and all the rest agreed. The problems in perceiving what would be just came mostly from "hard hearts" among the people.

Much of what we would consider mercy the Old Testament takes as a part of justice. According to Isaiah, God told the people of Israel, "Cease to do evil, learn to do good; seek justice, rescue the oppressed; defend the orphan, plead for the widow" (1:16–17). People were to harvest fields with justice, that is, they were to leave the edges standing so the poor would have something to eat. All this and more was just within the realm of justice. But Micah said God required the faithful to do justice and to love mercy. He spelled it out perhaps just in case there might be a question about the limits of justice.

Jesus extended the limits of justice. Christians were to go the extra mile—give the cloak and coat too. Christians were to keep on forgiving. Justice and mercy were to be extended to all.

In our own day, applications of the values of justice and mercy are readily apparent for Presbyterians who take the trouble to notice. Discrimination based on skin color, gender, and age cannot be just. Some ethical issues might be thorny, but one of the thorniest is basic justice for racial and ethnic minorities, refugees, women, older folks, children, and other groups. What Presbyterian can ignore the obvious need to seek justice for all these people? In fact, the great majority of us who are Presbyterians have tasted discrimination as members of one or more of these groups. The honest truth for us, however, is that most Americans who suffer the worst discrimination are not Presbyterians. We can love justice and seek mercy in their behalf.

Again, we Presbyterians affirm our growth in the body of Christ. If the Bible speaks clearly on matters of justice and mercy, and if we seek to do justice and to love mercy, we believe we can be led by God's Spirit from the more clear-cut issues into the more complex. This principle John Calvin and other Reformed theologians have repeated again and again, especially in matters of biblical interpretation: be guided by the simple and the clear. We have plenty of work to do if we begin with what we clearly know is fair, just, and merciful. In addition, we can rely upon our fellow Christians to provide us with guidance in responding to ethical issues.

## Caring and the Assembly

Many particular issues that call for us to love our neighbors do not have specific and obvious answers from the Bible. Our information on them seems mixed, and no clear word about right and wrong can be heard from responsible sources. In those cases, and in confronting issues of a very complex nature, we Presbyterians have a habit of investigating. Some of the time such work is done at the General Assembly level, both to draw on the greatest possible resources and also in order to speak an ethical word to the widest possible audience. The Assembly is charged, among other jobs, with the responsibility "to warn or bear witness against error in doctrine or immorality in practice in or outside the church" (*Book of Order*, G-13.0103p).

In previous years, Assemblies of various Presbyterian denominations have witnessed against many kinds of immorality and bad doctrine. Sometimes they have asked for the closing of fairs and expositions on Sunday, for the prohibition of liquor, for the withdrawal of armed forces from certain overseas lands, for ending support for oppressive governments (which some Assemblies have identified by name), and for the acceptance of refugees by Americans—all complicated statements that came from careful study and prayerful consideration.

These Assembly statements sometimes influence the actions of mission programs, home missions activities, and other organizations within the Presbyterian Church. They can also help people in local churches in their everyday decisions and actions. Some years ago, the Assemblies of the bodies that now constitute the Presbyterian Church (U.S.A.) took a stand against the advertising used by a major company selling dried milk in developing nations. The ads told mothers that their own milk was not as good for the babies. The actions of both Assemblies asked Presbyterians to cease buying products from that company until it changed its advertising in the new nations. The actions of the Assemblies affected buying patterns for church institutions. It also helped us individual Presbyterians know how to address the issue.

The statements of the Assemblies brought the matter to public attention, and the company took notice. Many Presbyterians disagreed with the statements of the Assemblies and the actions suggested. Many Presbyterians, on the other hand, began to talk about the need to boycott products from that company temporarily. The statements could not force any Presbyterian to cease buying the company's items. The statements did help us at Anchorage Presbyterian, however, for we discussed the matter in Sunday school on several occasions. Several of us probably became more interested in and knowledgeable about new nations as a result of the statements. In this matter, and in many more, I am convinced that Assemblies of the Presbyterian Church do help us focus on caring.

## Chapter Seven

# To Receive Baptism

She did not cry when her parents stood in front of the Anchorage congregation. Sarah Kelton, at two months old, simply looked around and took it all in. Bunnie and David, her parents, answered several questions about their faith and their willingness to bring Sarah up in the nurture and love of God. Then we in the congregation affirmed that we would also care for her as she matured. Finally, John Ames took Sarah in his arms and baptized her. The baby seemed a bit startled as John brought her down the aisle, telling her, "I want you to meet everyone." All the while, her grandparents beamed from the front pew.

About once a month we baptize infants in Williamsburg, just about the same as at Anchorage. About six times a year we baptize teenagers or adults. On each occasion people take vows, and we usually feel especially good as the sacrament takes place. We know baptism has been important for the church throughout the centuries, as has the Lord's Supper. We know Reformed teachings on it differ from some teachings of other churches, but what exactly are we doing in a baptism, and how does our understanding relate with that of other traditions?

## Baptism: A Sacrament

The early church began to develop a doctrine of baptism around the experiences Jesus shared with his disciples. Jesus himself had been baptized by John. He had instructed the disciples to baptize believers. From the time of Pentecost itself, apostles and disciples had baptized people. Philip even moved quickly to convert and baptize an Ethiopian, a minister in the court of the queen (Acts 8:26–40).

The early Christians' understanding of baptism broadened even further when Peter received a dream in Joppa. He saw all kinds of animals and heard a voice saying, "What God has made clean, you must not call profane." Peter responded to a request from Cornelius, a centurion of the Italian Cohort, to come to Caesarea. There Peter baptized Cornelius, a Roman soldier, with his household, when he perceived that Gentiles too had received the Holy Spirit (Acts 10).

With baptism, as with other special practices, Christians affirmed their continuity with the apostles and disciples of Jesus. In baptism, a person was initiated into the faith. In the Eastern Orthodox churches, emphasis was put on the preparation for resurrection. In the Western, Catholic churches, leaders emphasized the indelible new character of the believer and the beginning on the sacramental path. Baptism was viewed as the first of the seven sacraments upon which the faithful depended for nourishment in grace.

Reformed leaders in the sixteenth century such as Zwingli and Calvin tried to regain a biblical perspective on faith and do away with dependence on the sacramental system, but they took different views of the meaning of baptism. Zwingli considered it almost as much trouble as it was worth. Calvin saw how important it had been in the Gospel accounts of Jesus, how Jesus had commanded disciples to baptize people, and how the Acts church had practiced it. All Reformed leaders said, however, that in the sacraments nothing magical happened in a mechanical way. Baptism could not replace faith, which came from God.

Some of those who read their Bibles felt that any sacramentum, or "sacred thing," mistook the nature of the early church practice and the demands Christ gave. These reformers argued that Zwingli, Calvin, and Luther went only partway in a necessary reformation. They advocated the celebration of ordinances, things Christ told people to do, but they said sacraments were wrong.

Presbyterians since that time have taken a middle position on the sacraments—baptism and the Lord's Supper. We have continued to view baptism as a sacrament, but we have said sacraments in themselves do not save people or even help us to have more faith. In the words of the Directory for Worship, baptism "enacts and seals what the Word proclaims: God's redeeming grace offered to all people" (W-2.3006). The Directory for Worship is published as part of the *Book of Order*.

## Infant Baptism

Presbyterians baptize the children of believers, as do Catholics, Eastern Orthodox, Anglican, Lutheran, and several other Christian communions. According to Calvin, just as infants in Israel received circumcision, so children of Christians were to receive baptism (*Institutes* 4.14.24). It did not bother him that the Bible records no specific baptism of children. Calvin did point to the baptism of the household of Cornelius, but he did not argue that that meant God intended for the church to baptize all infants.

We Presbyterians say that baptism of infants "witnesses to the truth that God's love claims people before they are able to respond in faith" (W-2.3008b). We explain that "those presenting children for Baptism shall promise to provide nurture and guidance within the community of faith until the child is ready to make a personal profession of faith and assume the responsibility of active church membership" (W-2.3014).

Therefore, for Presbyterians the baptism of infants is a sign and seal of God's care for those particular children. It is also a promise taken by Christian parents and the wider church that the children will be educated in the faith, hopefully to receive the personal, saving knowledge of God at some future time. Presbyterians also like to quote Jesus, for he said that all must become like little children to receive the kingdom of God.

Not all Christians agree on infant baptism. Baptists are the most outspoken critics of this practice. They point to John the Baptist, to Jesus' receiving baptism as an adult, to the baptism of early Christians such as Cornelius. They say one must first repent, then believe, and then be baptized. Other Protestant communions, such as the Christian Church (Disciples of Christ) and the various Mennonite denominations, also practice believer baptism. They understand the practice of infant baptism as having arisen in state churches, where all had to be Christian whether or not they believed.

It makes little sense to argue, since both practices have biblical bases and long traditions. Moreover, it is easy for us Presbyterians to recognize other ways of interpreting the history as valid, even if they differ from our own. When Baptist or Christian Church (Disciples of Christ) persons join our denomination, we have no trouble recognizing their baptism as valid. Sometimes the reverse is not the case, and we need to understand the reluctance of many to accept our baptism as valid. We should also realize that no Presbyterian parents have to submit their infants for baptism.

David and Bunnie Kelton were Presbyterians before they married. They had no hesitation in presenting Sarah for baptism. On the other hand, several families I have known in Presbyterian congregations over the years have not asked for their children to be baptized. The Presbyterian Church has plenty of room for them too. Whether children are baptized or not, we have a responsibility to bring them up in the knowledge and love of God.

## Active Membership and Adult Baptism

At what is traditionally called "the age of discernment," children have the opportunity to make their own, personal profession of faith. When she was twelve years old, Sarah Kelton was invited to join a group of children her own age and receive intensive instruction from pastors and members of the session, though by then she and her family lived in a different city and belonged to a different Presbyterian congregation. She could have chosen to join an earlier group if she had wished. She might have refused altogether to participate in a group preparing for active church membership. She did accept the invitation and learned a lot about our church and about her part in it. In the congregations I have known, the groups in classes for confirmation and commissioning plan and lead a portion of Sunday worship at the end of their study as well as make their personal professions of faith.

Denominational mobility is a part of our modern society. People from other Reformed denominations and those from churches that recognize the Presbyterian Church as a part of God's family receive a letter of transfer if they have been active in the previous church. Those who have not been active elsewhere, though members and baptized in the Christian faith, simply make a reaffirmation of faith. Those who have been active in a church that does not issue letters of transfer to Presbyterian churches also reaffirm their faith.

Today in the United States, as in times past, many people have never been baptized. When a person joins the Presbyterian Church as a teenager or as an adult, that person receives believer baptism. He or she professes personal loyalty to Jesus Christ as Lord and Savior, as well as the willingness to participate in the life of the church, Christ's body. I have known several people reluctant to join the Presbyterian Church out of embarrassment that they have never been baptized. No sacramental time is more joyous than the baptism of a newly professing Christian, but we Presbyterians have been all too lazy in asking folks to come to church with us, to make a profession of faith in Jesus Christ, and to become members of Christ's body.

We can all grow in the knowledge and love of God. Christian education is vitally linked with baptism, both for infants and for adults.

### Education in the Faith

Sarah Kelton began Sunday school right away. At Anchorage Presbyterian Church and every other one to which I have belonged, a preschool class gives children an opportunity to hear Bible stories and play together with grownups. In successive classes, they learn more about the faith. Youth groups take trips together, and they share other activities. All these things are connected with the promises we make in baptism.

From the beginning of the Reformed tradition up to the present, Christian education has remained extremely important. The logic of its significance is very simple. If God expected each person to affirm or deny the gospel, and if saving knowledge had been given by the Holy Spirit to some people, then each person had to perceive the gospel—had to hear it. If no one could mediate the gospel, even though preachers could interpret it, and if the Bible offered everything necessary for saving knowledge, then everyone had to read the Bible. A portion of the task was translating the Bible into languages of the people. But another portion was in the teaching of everyone to read the Scriptures.

In places where Reformed faith flourished, literacy quickly became the rule among men (and sometimes even among women, although they usually had to learn in less formal settings). Other Protestant communions also emphasized education, and Catholics came to stress it for laypeople also, but none other quite as much as Reformed Christians.

When Sabbath schools (Sunday schools) began more than two centuries ago, they were for the children of the poor. The poor received no education and therefore could not read the Bible for themselves. Presbyterians cooperated with other Protestants to bring Sabbath schools to the needy as a service of evangelism and mission. Gradually, during the nineteenth century, Presbyterians came to use the Sabbath schools for their own children as well as for the poverty stricken. The same thing happened in other communions. The Sunday schools and church schools as we know them are rather recent organizations, existing from the latter part of the nineteenth century.

Presbyterian zeal for education extended to all realms. If, as we have seen, the creation is good, then knowledge of it is also good. Those in Reformed schools and colleges considered all kinds of learning to be important. The minister especially was expected to be learned in all kinds of disciplines. Harvard, Yale, Princeton, and other universities grew mainly from beginnings as Reformed seminaries for educating clergy and other church leaders. As the Presbyterians and Congregationalists grew apart, each group began its own colleges and seminaries. The Presbyterian ministers trained in these schools opened academies in their manses across the country where younger children could learn about God and the world.

Presbyterians cooperated in the public school movement in the nineteenth century despite the fact that they had developed a number of parochial schools. A part of their interest came from this commitment to teach each person to read. This would help each person to be accountable before God. It would help Presbyterians to keep their promises that children would grow in nurture and love of God.

Sunday schools, or church schools, have become a vital part of most congregations' corporate life. Some Presbyterians had already learned before the twentieth century that at different stages in growth and life people have different needs and abilities to learn about God and themselves. Today most Sunday schools have different lessons and activities for younger and older children, for those being confirmed in the church, and for adults. Some Presbyterians are also experimenting with activities that help different generations to learn from each other. The wide variety of kinds of education for the faith can offer growth for everyone.

Do Presbyterians have to actively support Christian education? There are some who do not, but at the same time, it is part and parcel of the promises we make in the baptism of both infants and adults. Church schools and all the other educational opportunities are occasions for us to learn about God, ourselves, and the mission of the church.

## Chapter Eight

# To Take Communion

George James almost always baked the bread for Communion at Anchorage. Sometimes he would bake crusted French bread, sometimes rye bread with lots of body, sometimes individual hot cross buns. George was an elder in the church for a number of years and liked to prepare for the Lord's Supper by baking bread. He said it gave him special time to think and pray.

At Ginter Park in Richmond we took the Lord's Supper with little squares of bread. At Williamsburg Presbyterian, we receive little strips of pita bread to dip into the cup (intinction) when we come to the front of the sanctuary row by row. At Highland I remember once in the Sunday school hour before the worship service celebrating with different breads and different methods of taking it.

A friend told of when he was in a church one summer where the pastor had stopped the day before to buy bread at the bakery without noticing what kind it was. It turned out to be spinach pesto bread, which sat in his hot car before the worship service. When he said the words of institution, "This is my body, broken for you," and broke the loaf, it oozed green gel.

George James knew that preparation for the Lord's Supper is extremely important in the Reformed tradition. Many Presbyterians do not make special preparation for the sacrament, though, and all of them are welcome at the table. In fact, in recent decades most Reformed bodies have stressed the open invitation "to all baptized believers and their children" to share in the Lord's Supper. To be Presbyterian means that we take Communion, but what does it mean in our faith?

## Communion: A Sacrament

Just as baptism remains a sacrament for Presbyterians, so does Communion. We believe that Jesus told members of the church to celebrate it, that he promised God's special presence as Communion is shared, and that Christians through the ages have continued faithfully to practice it. Three terms for us are synonymous: "Communion," "Lord's Supper," and "Eucharist" (from the Greek word for "grateful"). Jesus shared a Passover meal with his disciples. According to all the Gospels, it differed a bit from the regular Jewish feast. Jesus blessed the bread and the cup after supper and told his followers to share both (see Matt. 26:17–35; Mark 14:12–31; Luke 22:1–38; John 13:1–16:33). The Eucharist is also essential in the Roman Catholic Mass and in the liturgy of the Eastern Orthodox churches. Almost all kinds of Protestants celebrate Communion in some fashion.

Even before the sixteenth-century Reformation and the start of a Reformed tradition, Jan Hus in what is now the Czech Republic and John Wycliffe in England argued that the church should follow the Bible more closely in its teachings about Communion. Martin Luther, John Calvin, and other Reformers generally agreed, but they disagreed on what happened in the celebration. This disagreement, more than any other one issue, kept Protestants from unifying in the early years of the Reformation movement.

Following Calvin, Presbyterians have tried to steer a middle course between the "high" Communion theology of Catholics and Lutherans on the one hand, and the Protestants who consider it only an act of "remembering" and "hoping" on the other. Reformed creeds have stressed that it remains a sacrament, a holy event. However, it possesses no magic, and Presbyterians are not saved by taking it.

Early Presbyterians understood the church as universal, as the gathering of all Christians whether they believe Reformed teachings or not. It made sense for them to recognize God's work in all kinds of Communion celebrations. While Roman Catholics sometimes considered that a Presbyterian Communion service had no special power for the faithful, Presbyterians usually have not doubted God's work in the Mass so long as the believers do not depend on magic. By the same token, many times Baptists have demanded that Christians belong to a particular church in order to share Communion, thereby expressing doubt that Presbyterian Communion is a sacrament. Presbyterians have not hesitated to consider Baptist Communion true, and Baptist believers are welcome at Presbyterian Communion.

In Communion, the bread and the wine are signs that, according to Calvin, "represent for us the invisible food that we receive from the flesh and blood of Jesus Christ." God keeps feeding us in order for us to grow in our commitment to Christ. We obtain both assurance and delight from the sacrament—assurance of our eternal life and delight that God cares for us now and evermore (*Institutes* 4.17.1).

Serious students of the Presbyterian tradition today argue about the extent of Christ's "real presence" in the sacrament. Catholics and many Lutherans consider that Jesus Christ is present substantially in the sacrament itself. Presbyterians were generally thought to believe Christ was merely "represented" in the sacrament, but careful reading of Calvin's *Institutes* and other early Reformed theology shows that for them the "Spiritual Presence" they talked about was considered substantial. They wanted to guard against any mechanical understanding, but they believed that real communication of Christ's presence occurred.

## Presbyterian Practice

For many generations, Presbyterians and other Calvinists "fenced the table" for the Lord's Supper. Two ruling elders, or sometimes the minister, would go to each household during the week before a Communion service. They would examine all the members of the family who were full church members. Did they know important doctrines? Had they obeyed the law insofar as possible? Had they been faithful in worship and work? If the members passed, they would receive tokens for Communion. On the day of the service, after reading the Scripture and preaching an "action sermon" on the nature of the Holy Spirit's work in sanctifying the Lord's Supper, the minister would read Paul's words in 1 Corinthians 11:23–34. He would then invite all those with tokens to come forward and to sit at table. Those presenting tokens, sometimes only a small portion of the congregation, would be served Communion. All the other people would either watch from outside the fenced area or else go home.

These Presbyterians were paying special attention to the warning of 1 Corinthians 11:27–28 that if a person does not discern the body (i.e., understand what is happening), that person will incur God's judgment. Reformed churches took the Lord's Supper as primarily a "sealing ordinance" (and our Directory for Worship still calls it that—an occasion for sealing the faith of the believer in Communion with God through Christ's Spirit). During the nineteenth century, Presbyterians gradually came to emphasize Communion also as a "teaching ordinance," a time of learning in action the work of Christ through the Spirit.

Typically, Presbyterians celebrated the sacrament of Communion four times a year, though in some churches it was six times a year. Presbyterians would take the bread and the wine always in the context of worship. After Mr. Welch invented a process for keeping fermentation from occurring, and as the temperance movement became more powerful, over the objections of conservatives in many congregations grape juice became the "fruit of the vine" for most Presbyterians.

Today Presbyterian churches celebrate the Lord's Supper in different ways, with varying frequency. In some places, particularly in rural areas, quarterly Communion is still the habit. Many city churches take Communion the first Sunday of each month. Some congregations also offer eucharistic services weekly, perhaps in a small chapel early Sunday morning before regular worship. Youth conferences and retreats sometimes offer the Lord's Supper too.

The different customs reflect the varieties in Reformed theology today and the impact of the ecumenical movement.

Since the 1970s, Presbyterians have begun to permit baptized children to take Communion though they are not yet active church members. In addition, many congregations have begun to celebrate agape meals, based on the meals in the early church similar to Communion. A word about each of these new practices is in order.

## Communion for Children

John Calvin long ago said that the Lord's Supper is "by nature incomprehensible" because it remains a mystery how Christ is united with the faithful. As Presbyterians have become more interested again in his theology, and as we have come in contact with other Christian traditions more fully, we have moved in recent years to permit baptized children to share in the sacrament. One might say we became more modest in our claims about our own knowledge of what takes place in Communion. One could also say that we began paying greater attention to some other passages in the Bible, particularly to the words of Jesus: "Let the little children come to me, and do not stop them, for it is to such as these that the kingdom of heaven belongs" (Matt. 19:14). In addition to these reasons, another is probably that the same movement is going on in most Protestant churches that baptize children.

The *Book of Order* says that a baptized member of a particular church who "has not made a profession of faith in Jesus Christ as Lord and Savior" is "entitled to the pastoral care and instruction of the church, and to participation in the Sacrament of the Lord's Supper" (G-5.0301). All the members of the congregation cooperate in providing this instruction and understanding for the children—not just the parents. At Anchorage Presbyterian Church I first noticed that some adults from time to time did not take it. I have also observed the same in other congregations. I suppose the hesitation comes from the tradition, when it was considered just a "sealing ordinance" and not also a "teaching ordinance."

I think those of us who sought the changes and enjoy the freedom of baptized children to take Communion need to understand the feelings of others with different perspectives. After all, we acknowledge that Communion offers no magical power for believers to help them in being saved. On the other hand, people hesitant to take Communion in times of feeling guilty or who are full of remorse, as well as those who will not permit baptized children on the road to active membership to take Communion, may need to gain understanding also.

## Agape Meals and Other Celebrations

A number of Presbyterian congregations now celebrate agape meals from time to time. Either in conjunction with a family night supper, or on its own, an agape meal can be inspirational and full of good worship. An agape meal, like early Christian love feasts, involves a group of Christians sharing bread and perhaps other foods as well. Sometimes the use of symbolic foods and numbers helps remind us of certain events from the ministry of Jesus—the use of five loaves of bread and two fish, for example. When we gather for an agape meal, we sing and pray. We also can learn about one another in an informal setting.

I mention the agape meal at this point because it is not for us a sacrament. We Presbyterians share several kinds of celebrations that are extremely important and full of religious meaning but are not sacraments. Historically, Wednesday night prayer meetings have been a part of congregational life in many local churches. Family night suppers, too, have been special occasions for Presbyterians in all parts of the country. Weddings and funerals are significant worship times, of special meaning to church families and to the wider congregation (see chapter 11). In Memphis, Louisville, Richmond, Williamsburg, and probably in many other cities across the country, Presbyterians from many congregations are gathering weekly at a central location for Bible study. These times all bear God's grace as surely as if they were sacramental. Baptism and the Lord's Supper differ only in the fact that Christ promised to be present as these sacraments take place.

In our Reformed tradition, especially among the Puritans, there has been a strain of faith that has considered every day the Lord's Day, every Sunday an Easter. Many Presbyterians continue to share this spirit that all days are holy, all services of worship the occasion for the special presence of God. Some Presbyterians on good ethical bases shy from celebrations—especially from fancy ones. Others, from various backgrounds and with good reasons also, really enjoy the Christian seasons, the special celebrations such as agape meals, and other such events. I am delighted that in this area of church life we Presbyterians have many different styles and expectations. There is latitude, and Presbyterians are required only to pay special attention to the two sacraments, whatever our other preferences and habits.

## Chapter Nine

# To Belong to the Church

Some years ago, Harriet Hilley, then a senior in high school, went from Anchorage Presbyterian Church to the Republic of Zaire to deliver an airplane. She and another American Presbyterian represented the young people from across the church who had contributed to buy the plane. They gave it to the Protestant church in Zaire so that their evangelists and medical personnel could reach people in outlying areas of the country where roads were particularly poor. These medical and evangelistic ministers could bring the gospel and serve the needs of people in other way too, because Harriet and lots of other teenagers helped.

We Presbyterians are members of a universal church. Examples of our Christian solidarity are all over the place, if we stop to notice them. When he visited the United States, for example, I took Joong-Eun Kim, his wife, Gwi Yub, and their son Hyong Woo to a birthday celebration at Mt. Sterling Presbyterian Church. Kim is now president of the Presbyterian College and Seminary in Seoul, Korea, and Gwi Yub is a specialist in Christian education. In the regular adult Sunday school class preceding the special worship service celebrating the event, the teacher began to explore accounts in the books of Samuel about the early monarchy. Kim, whose specialty is Old Testament, explained about the various ways in which the people of Israel viewed the king—a hope, a threat, a promise from God, a foretelling of a real messiah, and so forth. Here was a Korean teacher and minister, educated in both Korea and Switzerland, sharing with American Christians words from the Old Testament that all of us care about.

Though not so apparent all the time, our life in the church universal is a real part of our being Presbyterians. Previous chapters have mentioned some formal aspects of this life. Consider, though, the belief we voice in "the communion of saints." More than a formal link with others in Presbyterian churches across the world and with all other Christians, we have a spiritual link. No wonder one of the most beloved hymns is "Blessed be the tie that binds / our hearts in Christian love; / the fellowship of kindred minds / is like to that above" (John Fawcett, 1782). No wonder a Communion service with fellow Christians from across a region, nation, or world seems particularly powerful and moving!

As we affirm our Christianity in the Presbyterian strain of it, we are reminded of both the opportunities in our local situations and of the ways we claim responsibility in the worldwide church of Jesus Christ. In addition, we see the part that corporate prayer plays in our religious life.

### Member of the Whole Church

Belief and practice really do form a single fabric. In the nineteenth and early twentieth centuries, when the missionary movement among Presbyterians had begun in earnest, congregations would thrill to the reports of those sent from their number to serve in other lands. I honestly think that vitality for American Christians came in large measure from the joy shared in helping take the gospel to other lands.

One of my own favorite stories recounts the work of William Henry Sheppard and William McCutchen Morrison in Africa. Sheppard, an early African American minister in the Presbyterian Church, grew up in Waynesboro, Virginia, and attended Hampton Institute and what became Stillman College. Morrison, who graduated from Louisville Seminary, translated the gospel into the languages of several different tribal groups along the Congo River. As they evangelized, they encountered the oppression of

King Leopold of Belgium, who forced exorbitant taxes from the people and whose representatives in the colonial government permitted torture of tribes that would not or could not pay. Sheppard and Morrison wrote to Christians in the United States and elsewhere, especially to Presbyterians, and the two missionaries were sued for libel by the king. Their trial in a newly established World Court enabled the atrocities to be documented for the media. As a result, the gross oppression was diminished, even as members of the tribes learned about Jesus Christ.

I cannot help but believe that Harriet Hilley, William Henry Sheppard, William McCutchen Morrison, and all the rest, in various ways, have helped Christians in America to cooperate with Christians in Central Africa. We are linked with Christians there in a special way. I take particular interest in Congo (formerly Zaire) and its churches in part because other members of the wider church have been and will be drawing my interest and prayers there.

Think today of Christians in Korea, many of whom are Presbyterians. They are bringing the gospel to colleagues in ways somewhat different from our own. They emphasize small-group Bible study, which might be a strategy that we Americans could better use. They also stand up when necessary to proclaim the rights of Christian people and other citizens to gather and speak freely. Some of the Christian leaders have spent time in jail. International bodies that thoroughly investigate reports of oppression say Christians were tortured there; certainly many were martyred in what is now North Korea. We American Christians are linked closely with them as they evangelize, as they witness, and as they make inroads to provide care for North Korean Christians.

We American Presbyterians are linked, through the work of Christ's Spirit, to the faithful throughout the world, for similar stories can be told about Presbyterian missionaries and faithful Christians from among the converts in China, Cuba, Brazil, Iraq, Lebanon, Ethiopia, Egypt, Cameroon, and many other locations of emergent or now-thriving churches. This identification causes us sorrow when others suffer, and we receive joy when others experience it. Naturally, we cannot know about all the other Christian communities and works of charity. Through international missions and service organizations we help others and they help us. No wonder Presbyterians have been supporters of the World Council of Churches (WCC), the National Council of Churches USA, and Church World Service. No wonder we also are supporters of the World Alliance of Reformed Churches (WARC), an organization of many Presbyterian, Congregationalist, and other so-called Calvinist bodies. That body is planning to merge with another, smaller group of churches that earlier declined to join the WARC. In June 2010, the World Alliance of Reformed Churches and the Reformed Ecumenical Council will form the World Communion of Reformed Churches.

Sometimes when Christians in other lands have differing perspectives on needs and ways to help, American Christians have been quick to criticize such organizations. No doubt the World Council of Churches makes mistakes, just as we believe our own General Assembly is capable of error, and just as we believe we ourselves are not perfect in this life. I personally take some solace in the knowledge that the WCC, in service work, meets the needs of starving people in many countries. I am delighted that a portion of the money I contribute to the Presbyterian Church, be it ever so small, is used by Church World Service.

The command of Jesus for Christians to be "witnesses" all over the world was very clear: "You will be my witnesses in Jerusalem, in all Judea and Samaria, and to the ends of the earth" (Act 1:8). Sometimes I think I'm in Jerusalem, sometimes in Judea, sometimes in Samaria, and sometimes in the uttermost parts of the world. Wherever I am, I know that in all these places I am to be a witness. People in your congregation and in the ones where I worship and work, like folks throughout America, are now traveling all over the world. Some such as Bob Fritts in our Williamsburg congregation, who was once ambassador to Ghana, serve in official capacities. Others, such as Bob and Nancy Archibald, who both work at the College of William and Mary, recently went to Congo as volunteers. Many others of us find ourselves in other countries for work or play or both. It seems that all of us, whether we actually travel to various countries in person or whether our representatives are there, share in this worldwide witness—on a scale never before realized in human history.

We have many responsibilities as Christians, both as we go to various lands and as we participate in worldwide mission and service activity. Yet all Presbyterians do not agree on ways in which we can witness. I am reminded of the time my wife, Carolyn, and I helped a nurse in a well-baby clinic in Congo. We served two lines of mothers who had brought their babies for anti-malaria pills. My wife and I simply gave the mothers and infants pills. The nurse, however, said to each mother in the other line in Tshiluba, "This is from the church for you and for your baby. Go in the name of Jesus Christ." It seemed to be a microcosm of Christian witness that day, some of us explicitly mentioning Christ and telling people about the faith while others of us witnessing by action without necessarily saying the words about Jesus Christ. We Presbyterians have a history of witnessing in both ways. Certain ones of us are more inclined to one or another style of Christian witness. Our belonging to the worldwide church rightly includes both areas of witness (and many more), as we travel for work and play in various countries and as we participate with those who share missions here and abroad.

## Member of the Local Church

The Christian community is not just worldwide. It is also very near at hand. We take care lest we act like a character in one of George Bernard Shaw's plays who went forever to meetings in behalf of people on the other side of the globe while her own family fell to pieces. Our own families and our church families deserve attention as we consider what it means to be a Presbyterian. As we have seen from the illustrations within Anchorage Presbyterian and other congregations, many of us have different interests and gifts.

At Highland Presbyterian in Louisville, for example, there are Stephen Ministers, highly trained for one-on-one ministry to people who are ill or grieving. There are deacons who visit the sick and needy sometimes but more frequently bring their needs to the attention of the whole church, and there are members who take decorated Christmas trees to those who are not able to set up and decorate trees themselves. There are volunteers who visit new members and others who are homebound, and there are elders who take Communion to those in nursing homes. The pastors also visit when their presence is needed, and they visit those they think need to be challenged to serve in new efforts. Then there is Mary Henry, who says she does not like to belong to organized efforts to visit and see people, so she just goes where she thinks she should to help. I am certain there are many others at Highland who do as Mary Henry does. Among all the groups and individuals there is a sense of cooperation; as a result, Highland has what might be termed a "thick" culture of hospitality.

We Presbyterians belong to the church universal in local congregations. In addition to the beliefs we share about this fact (discussed in chapter 4), we share also a mutual dependence. Sometimes I am emotionally moved by the sense that we all are together what none of us could be individually. When a member of the congregation needs help, people pitch in and help. It may not be the same people every time, for different ones of us are closer to some families and individuals than to others. There seem to be some "all-purpose players" on our congregational teams, who single out people not being cared for and then go and care for those folks.

Again as at every point, we Presbyterians remember that church people are sinful people, even as we serve God and God's creation. At Anchorage, Highland, Ginter Park, and Williamsburg, as in every congregation, many folks do not seem to bear their share of the load. Many others could do more than they do. "There is no one who is righteous, not even one" (Rom. 3:10). Though Presbyterians are not forced to do a certain amount of work in a local church, the nexus between that congregation and a particular member's own gifts quickly become apparent. It seems to be a direct responsibility of Presbyterians to share in the life of a congregation even as we share in the worldwide church.

## Time, Talents, Money

A traditional way we Presbyterians have expressed responsibility has been in terms of giving back to God our time, talents, and money. As we recognize that all life, faith, love, and other gifts come from God, so we recognize our responsibility to render back a portion of what has been given us in these areas.

Reformed Christians have remembered that the tithe was extremely important in the life of the people of Israel. Though Jesus lived, died, and rose, fulfilling a law we could not fulfill, we see the giving back to God of one-tenth of God's gifts to us as a good starting point for Christian living. Presbyterians in other generations and in other cultures today use the tithe as a natural yardstick.

Others point to differing needs of people during different stages of living and argue that a more flexible measure is better. A person could leave a portion of an estate for the work of the church, for example. In whatever way possible, we Presbyterians need to share in the work of the church with the giving (or rendering back) of significant portions of our money.

Perhaps the giving of time and talents is even more important. Almost every congregation possesses many people of immense talent and skill. Think of what the local church could be if each gave according to skill and interest, both to the local church and to the universal church. Presbyterian churches in other lands may be looking right now, as many usually are, for a man or woman willing to be a printer, a farmer, a business consultant, an architect, a medical technician, a teacher, a nurse, or a minister for a period of time. A man, woman, couple, or family can serve another Christian body or an ecumenical ministry for a particular period of time today. Some churches want that kind of service especially. Again, our congregation and every other I know would love to have more help from members skilled in particular areas of ministry. To be a Presbyterian is to consider with the church what talents and what commitments of time can be used for the needs of the church.

### Prayer

Our prayer life is another part of belonging to the church, as it is a part of corporate worship. Our spiritual links with other Christians in our locale and across the earth are shared in our prayers. As Presbyterians, we have a tradition of praying together, but we let no priest or minister do all of our praying for us. Corporate prayer is supplemented with private prayer.

Jesus had many things to say about prayer, such as the fact that we should be modest in our words and phrases (Matt. 6:5–6). He also gave an example of prayer, which we Protestants follow in different fashion from the way Catholics do. In chapter 14 we will consider the practice of prayer in more depth.

## Chapter Ten

# To Obey the Law

Yes, we are working rather hard on the sewer lines." Peyton Hoge, the mayor of Anchorage, was talking to our Issues Class in Sunday school. He was a member of the church when we attended it and periodically was invited to talk with us about the major community issues, the proposal to reorganize county government, and other political matters. Many members of the congregation lived in the little city of Anchorage, but even those of us who did not reside in the community itself saw the importance of his presence with us. Did the police need a pay increase? Was the bridge unsafe across one of the town's creeks? What issues would face the state during the coming year? Peyton was knowledgeable about all these things, and we fellow Presbyterians sensed our need to know about them and encourage him in leadership.

Peyton Hoge was not the only politician who talked with us in that church. From time to time our local state representative would come to a church dinner, or the candidates for political office would be invited to debate for a church forum. Most of us Presbyterians see responsible citizenship in the nation and community as a part of our Christian commitment. Very frequently sparks will fly when some of us argue for a better school system, while others of us seek no new taxes. We do not all agree on other issues—food stamps, aid for college students, the welfare structure, criteria for election of officials, and so forth—yet we are willing to listen to knowledgeable people describe their points of view.

At subsequent congregations in which I have worked and worshiped, similar attention is given to listening and learning about civil society and about the issues important to those particular communities. At Ginter Park, a long-lived and popular Sunday school class named for an elder in that congregation, the Aubrey Brown Peace Forum, attracts people who are not even members of the church. At Williamsburg's "Men's Breakfast (Women Welcome Too)," held on several Saturdays each year, politicians and other public figures discuss issues with us.

I would venture to say that all of us Presbyterians want to obey the law. More than that, we want to belong to a civil society as mature and active citizens. What is it about the Reformed faith that fosters such commitment? Is it a different stance from that of other Christian bodies in America?

## Render to Caesar

Historically, Christians have been "good citizens" in most lands since the time of Constantine. Jesus, frequently quoted on the subject, said, "Give therefore to the emperor the things that are the emperor's, and to God the things that are God's" (Matt. 22:21). He was speaking about paying a province's governor in the coins that the Roman Empire minted. Since early in the fourth century, Christians in the West have been the favored people of the state almost all the time. When barbarians overthrew Rome, they may have destroyed a part of the civilization, but they were as much Christians as the people they overthrew had been. When the Reformation occurred, various parties may have called each other "pagans," but all at least were nominally Christian.

Reformed leaders in Switzerland, France, England, Scotland, the Netherlands, areas of what is now Germany, and elsewhere wanted their faith to be the established faith of the realm. Seeking to maintain the favored status of Calvinism in several New England colonies, Puritans zealously guarded the "city set on a hill." When early Presbyterians came to America from Scotland and Northern Ireland, they expected to obtain favored status for their faith in the new world.

Since the Revolutionary War and the forming of voluntary religious denominations—Protestant, Catholic, Jewish, and others—the United States has experimented with this new pattern of church-state relationships. We Presbyterians today in the United States are heirs of all this history, and it has a bearing on our thinking about politics as on social responsibility. Many scholars argue that our Calvinism has an effect on our economic behavior also.

Since at least the fifth century, we Christians have perceived ourselves as belonging to two "cities," mutually dependent yet not identical. One is the city of "human beings," in which nothing is perfect. Yet in the human city, life can be more just at certain times than at others. The other city is the city of God, in which we belong but do not yet live. The "realm of Caesar" has been interpreted as a body in which we have citizenship, which is quite different from the situation in which Jesus and the disciples spoke about politics. The "realm of God" has its beginning in the church universal, though the believers of earth are not the same thing as the "communion of saints" in heaven.

Thomas Jefferson coined the phrase "a wall of separation," and this barrier has partially existed between church and state, with the realms sometimes even being seen as mutually exclusive. Occasionally even Presbyterians have seen the spiritual as unrelated to the political, especially as the doctrine of the "spirituality of the church" developed in the South. That phrase came to be used widely in the late nineteenth century. Some Presbyterians have gone even further, arguing along with Mennonites and some Baptists that Christians should shun the world, which is a "vale of tears." A few have refused to vote in political elections because the United States has not recognized Jesus Christ as Lord of the land.

For the most part, however, Presbyterians have been vitally involved in the duties of citizenship. Most joined the ranks of the revolutionaries at the time of Independence (though some good

Presbyterians sided with Great Britain and even fought against the Revolutionaries). A Presbyterian, John Witherspoon, was the only member of the clergy to sign the Declaration of Independence. A member of the British Parliament who was visiting the war effort wrote home to say it was a "Presbyterian rebellion." Since the formation of the United States, Presbyterians have served in almost every elective office in the land. Several presidents, including Woodrow Wilson and Dwight Eisenhower, have been active Presbyterians. In the 111th Congress, ten senators and thirty-three members of the House of Representatives belong to the PC(USA). Numerous members of the Supreme Court, members of Congress far out of proportion to the denominational numbers, and scores of governors have over the years been Presbyterians.

Presbyterians by and large have viewed the civil government as a separate realm from the church. However, we have generally seen the law as a good influence on civil life. We have considered that governments should protect the freedom of persons to gather in expression of religious beliefs. We have considered that churches should not control governments either. Rather, because all institutions keep a degree of human sinfulness, systems of checks and balances within the church, within the state, and between church and state are healthy.

In earlier decades Roman Catholics did not usually support such a position on church and state, coming frequently to America from nations in which a state church had existed. When American Catholics did speak up for religious freedom, they sometimes received rebukes from Rome. More recently, Catholics have become quite open in thinking about the legitimate independence of church and state. Lutherans, Methodists, and Episcopalians have also shared similar positions to those of Presbyterians. Some Baptists, especially members of the more closed associations, in which other Christians are seen as unworthy of salvation, seem to think the church should dominate political affairs. American Baptist Convention members, most Southern Baptists, and almost all National Baptists stand in the tradition of desiring separation of church and state, some more forcefully than Presbyterians.

### Third Use of the Law

Reformed church people traditionally have shared a particular viewpoint on the usefulness of the law, especially the Ten Commandments, for Christians and for all society. John Calvin, whose views on the uses of the law differed from those of other Reformers, said that God gave the law for three reasons: (1) to bring "the elect to salvation" into repentance by the work of the Holy Spirit; (2) to restrain those who seek to do evil and care little or nothing for justice or mercy; and (3) to teach the godly "the nature of the Lord's will" (*Institutes* 2.7.12).

Martin Luther, Anabaptist leaders, and most others who came to be Protestants outside the camp of Calvin merely contrasted law and gospel. God gave the law, which the people of Israel and everyone else broke. Then God gave Jesus Christ to save those who depended on him rather than in their ability to keep the law. Luther set law against gospel. The law only worked to restrain evildoers and to provoke repentance.

Calvin said that law continues to function positively for believers as a teacher for us all. This emphasis on the "third use of law" traditionally distinguishes Presbyterians and other Reformed Christians from the rest of Protestantism.

Calvin followed the teachings of the apostle Paul in this understanding, as Luther did in contrasting law and gospel. In Galatians, to name just one example of Calvin's use of the Bible, Paul said, "For the whole law is summed up in a single commandment, 'You shall love your neighbor as yourself.' If, however, you bite and devour one another, take care that you are not consumed by one another" (Gal. 5:13–15). Paul said a bit later, "Bear one another's burdens, and in this way you will fulfill the law of Christ" (Gal. 6:2). Calvin also followed the statement of Jesus that he had come to fulfill the law rather than to abolish it.

No wonder, then, that John Calvin and others after him in our tradition have paid so much attention to the Ten Commandments. The classic confessions of the Reformed churches, such as the Heidelberg Catechism, the Westminster Confession, and the Larger and Shorter Catechisms, spell out each of the commandments, and the Westminster Standards say what each means in part. Early Reformed congregations in each Lord's Day service took the time to recite all the commandments. After all, when that rich young man had asked Jesus about being saved, what was Jesus' first reply? Being a Christian among early Presbyterians meant being delivered from dependence on the law for salvation. The work of the Holy Spirit in the life of believers enabled followers to come closer to obedience.

This attention to the law as a teacher for the righteous and for the redeemed naturally related to certain civil laws for Presbyterians. Reformed Christians, for example, heard the commandment to "remember the Sabbath day, and keep it holy" (Exod. 20:8). In the sixteenth century, Reformed Christians began to punish "Sabbath breakers" with some harshness. That idea of a Puritan Sabbath, in which the civil government made rules about keeping "the Lord's Day," has been very important in the United States also. Even today some states forbid the sale of alcohol on Sundays during certain hours, and many local governments have additional rules about activities on Sundays. All these "blue laws," more important just a few decades ago than they are today, came from a sense of the power of the moral law in society. Scholars today are studying the impact of the "Calvinist worldview" in forming American character. Some say that no other idea has been more significant than this worldview, though most people today do not recognize its source.

## Higher Law

As almost all other religious people, Presbyterians recognize that human law has limitations. Even if well designed and well enforced, human law will not keep perfect justice. Nor can it inject mercy into the social system. Frequently human laws are less than well designed and are enforced unfairly. Christians recognize that God's law transcends human law. Presbyterians seem to be more willing than most Christians to obey "higher law," given our beliefs about the sinfulness of all people and the duty of the faith.

Paul spoke of the "higher law" as the law of love, "a still more excellent way" (1 Cor. 12:31). He had been willing to suffer imprisonment for his mission work, which went against the law as interpreted by local magistrates. Indeed, the whole Christian tradition is full of people standing for higher law against oppressive human laws, just as the tradition is full of Christians protesting against their colleagues who claimed "higher law" as a basis of action.

Every Christian working in behalf of revolution, including Presbyterians fighting for an independent United States of America, has claimed allegiance to "the higher law of God." Over the years different issues have become part of the Presbyterian claim for the authority of "higher law." During the struggle for Prohibition, teetotal Presbyterians sometimes shut down taverns illegally in the name of higher law. During the civil rights struggle, some Presbyterians disobeyed laws enforcing segregation. Today Presbyterians may invoke "higher law" in withholding taxes meant to support nuclear weapons development or a war not declared by the U.S. Congress. In each case, other Presbyterians have objected that these people were "disobedient," "disloyal," or downright traitors to their countries.

While from our Reformed tradition we can see clearly our responsibility to obey the law, we see also the tradition of civil disobedience as a part of that duty sometimes. Perceiving the nature of obedience is not simple for Presbyterians or for any Christians who understand our dual citizenship—in the city of God and the human city. Frequently we Presbyterians of different attitudes and various backgrounds have been intolerant of one another. Some of us chafe at the impatience of others. Others of us feel the call of particular visions of justice and mercy. Can there be room for our differences as we seek to obey the law? All Presbyterians recognize that none of us possesses perfect righteousness. We all "see through a glass, darkly" (1 Cor. 13:12 KJV) as we try to be obedient.

*Chapter Eleven*

# To Anticipate the Kingdom

The memorial service at Anchorage for Helen Sherrill was a special occasion. We gathered, young and old, led by Pastor John Ames and Edgar Houghton, a pastor long retired. We wanted to give thanks for her life and to share remembrances of her with members of her family. Helen had been a member of Anchorage Presbyterian for several decades, and her husband had attended faithfully with her for years before his death. She was a pioneering specialist in early childhood development, and she had given untold energy to the efforts of the congregation in Christian education. She had also been a tireless worker in behalf of the neighboring Bellewood Home for Children.

When women were eligible for ordination as elders, she was one of the first elected in the whole denomination. Mostly, though, she was a faithful Christian person, rearing children in love and nurture, caring for those in need, and greeting strangers warmly. When Carolyn and I first visited Anchorage Church, she welcomed us warmly.

Helen lived in anticipation of the kingdom of God, to which she already hoped to belong while she served among us. When she died, we felt her loss keenly. Why, even in the nursing home she had retained good humor and sought to help those around her! However, in the assurance of our faith granted by the Holy Spirit, we knew that Helen Sherrill had joined fully the kingdom to which she already belonged. Our service of worship was indeed a witness to the resurrection. We joined her children, other family, and longtime friends in affirming the power of Christ's resurrection, Helen's, and our own.

In our affirming the authority of the Bible and in our following the confessions of Reformed communities, we Presbyterians believe that God will care for us after death as God has provided for us through life. Jesus Christ said many things about the nature of eternal life, and the creeds of the church have mentioned resurrection also. Assurance of salvation, according to John Calvin, was one of the benefits of Christ in our behalf. God's predestination of the elect was another. All these beliefs together seek to describe our glimpses into the reality beyond earthly, human life. All are important for Presbyterians.

## Eternal Life in the Bible

"The LORD is my shepherd, I shall not want. . . . Even though I walk through the darkest valley, I fear no evil; for you are with me" (Ps. 23:1, 4). Long before the coming of Jesus, the people of Israel considered God's providence eternal. Psalms from different periods in Israel's history attest to the continuity in their faith.

Jesus did teach more about eternal life, and he specifically told his disciples that he would provide for them: "Very truly, I tell you, whoever believes has eternal life" (John 6:47). Jesus said to Martha, "I am the resurrection and the life. Those who believe in me, even though they die, will live" (John 11:25). The narratives in which each of these sayings occur tell about life eternal, and resurrection as a part of it.

Jesus also spoke frequently about the "kingdom of heaven." Many of the parables tell about what the kingdom is like— a sower of good seeds who separates wheat from tares after an enemy sowed weed seeds in the crop (Matt. 13:24–30), a grain of mustard seed (13:31–32), leaven in bread (13:33), and a merchant of fine pearls finding one worth everything (13:45–46). The kingdom of heaven, as Jesus described it, was not altogether otherworldly. He said it began in the hearts of people, and life on earth had much to do with it. On the other hand, the kingdom of heaven was not just a part of this world. It had to do with eternity, with life everlasting, and with resurrection.

Jesus addressed his disciples with a promise: "Do not let your hearts be troubled. Believe in God, believe also in me. In my Father's house are many dwelling places. If it were not so, would I have told you that I go to prepare a place for you? And if I go and prepare a place for you, I will come again and will take you to myself, so that where I am you may be also" (John 14:1–3).

The early church heard the promise, and some thought Jesus would return within their lifetimes to bring his kingdom of heaven. It gave many pause when believers died. Paul wrote several of his epistles at least in part to meet this situation. To the Corinthians, for example, Paul said the gospel depended on the resurrection of Jesus: "For I handed on to you as of first importance what I in turn had received, that Christ died for our sins in accordance with the scriptures, and that he was buried, and that he was raised on the third day in accordance with the scriptures" (1 Cor. 15:3–4). If Christ had arisen, Paul argued, how could people claim there was no resurrection? If Christ had not been raised, then the gospel was false at its core. "But in fact Christ has been raised from the dead, the first fruits of those who have died" (1 Cor. 15:20).

Sometimes the Bible tells a little about the nature of eternal life. There will be no giving and taking in marriage, Jesus told one person who was trying to trick him (Mark 12:25). Paul said, "There are both heavenly bodies and earthly bodies" (1 Cor. 15:40). There will be a judgment, according to many writers portraying the sayings of Jesus. Life will be quite different. Apocalyptic books, such as the book of Revelation, give a gorgeous picture:

> Then I saw a new heaven and a new earth; for the first heaven and the first earth had passed away, and the sea was no more. And I saw the holy city, a new Jerusalem, coming down out of heaven from God, prepared as a bride adorned for her husband. . . . And God himself will be with them;

he will wipe away every tear from their eyes. Death will be no more; mourning and crying and pain will be no more. (Rev. 21:1–4)

The book of Revelation, as other apocalyptic books, speaks in symbols more vague than those in other parts of the Bible. It speaks of a heaven with pearl gates and gold streets, choruses of angels, and the fall of cosmic evil. But all language is symbolic to some degree, and Reformed readers of the Bible have usually been hesitant to say too much about the nature of resurrection, eternal life, immortality of the soul, or the rest of the results of salvation. Indeed, most Christians have remained modest about such matters, and with good reason.

## The Resurrection of the Dead

In that early statement of belief known to us as the Nicene Creed, the church said simply that Jesus "rose again in accordance with the Scriptures; he ascended into heaven and is seated at the right hand of the Father." Jesus "will come again in glory to judge the living and the dead, and his kingdom will have no end." The creed concludes with another simple sentence: "We look for the resurrection of the dead, and the life of the world to come." Subsequent creeds have not added much by way of spelling out the nature of resurrection or life in the kingdom of heaven.

From its very beginning, Christianity moved into a society in which Greek ideas dominated thought and Greek language shared with Latin the center stage for communication. As in the case of church debates about the nature of Jesus Christ as divine and human, in the case of life after death different cultures used various expressions to describe it. Greek thought generally focused on immortality of the soul. Such eternal life had been taught by philosophers centuries before the coming of Christian missionaries. Soon the resurrection of the body and the immortality of the soul were seen as the same thing.

Recently, with language study and with modern philosophy, many have contrasted the two expressions. Some say Christianity teaches resurrection of the body, not immortality of the soul. Others now say that both are biblical expressions of the mystery concerning life everlasting. I can see little difference in the expressions, although perhaps "resurrection of the body" does give a bit more of a sense that the whole person is involved in life eternal. Frankly, I wish we had additional vocabulary to express the mystery and anticipate the reality of it.

Along with Christians of all stripes, Presbyterians use many expressions, including "pass over Jordan," "be with God," and "see face-to-face." All these and many others are fine biblical metaphors to talk about a life to come. I am delighted that our communion does not become preoccupied with speculation about the nature of eternal life, and such an attitude seems to be in harmony with John Calvin's.

Calvin used the image of God talking in a kind of baby talk to us, not just in matters about resurrection but also in the whole Bible. The varieties of images in the Bible, said Calvin, did not prove that God changed. Rather, they showed God's accommodation to our limited capacity for knowledge and faith (*Institutes* 2.11.13). In other words, when the people considered the world flat, with heaven above them, God's accommodation involved the use of images that told divine truth in that worldview. Our worldview of a solar system in one galaxy among other such clusters of spheres means that God's truth comes to us in language we can fathom too. All the same, Presbyterians have many different conceptions of the nature of eternal life, resurrection, and even of salvation. We can hold them well without necessarily inflicting them on others. Our modesty in this area of doctrine becomes our situation as a small portion of a human population on one of the medium planets in a rather small solar system. We can affirm the teachings of the Bible and the tradition in which we are sharing all the same.

## Predestination

Though Presbyterians today do not usually brag about "our doctrine," it still seems necessary with the mention of Calvin, eternal life, and the Bible's teachings to say something about predestination. After all, that is the first of the Presbyterian idiosyncrasies, is it not?

The first thing to note about predestination is that it did not originate with John Calvin, the Westminster Confession, or sesquipedalian (i.e., users of big words) ministers. It comes from the Bible. Paul, in the very middle of the Epistle to the Romans, says that we know "in everything God works for good with those who love him, who are called according to his purpose." Then he goes on to use the word: "For those whom [God] foreknew he also predestined to be conformed to the image of his Son. . . . And those whom he predestined he also called; and those whom he called he also justified; and those whom he justified he also glorified" (Rom. 8:28–30). In the Epistle to the Ephesians Paul says God had blessed us, "just as he chose us in Christ before the foundation of the world to be holy and blameless before him in love" (Eph. 1:4). Paul did not think he was saying anything unusual either, for he and the rest of the early Christians believed they had been predestined to follow Jesus Christ.

Moreover, through the history of the church until the eighteenth century at least, few if any leaders had failed to mention this important doctrine, much less openly deny it. Thomas Aquinas, who influenced Catholic theology perhaps more than anyone else, said almost everything Calvin did about predestination. Thus, it was not an innovation among Reformed Christians.

Second, Calvin considered predestination to be just one of the "benefits of Jesus Christ for us," alongside prayer, resurrection, and several other things. Calvin recognized the trap in dwelling on predestination, but he said he felt compelled to follow the Bible. What Calvin evidently took for a word of comfort, a solace when things were particularly difficult, some Reformed thinkers after him emphasized a lot. Calvin spoke more modestly about predestination than did his successors. He said Jesus had talked about sheep and goats at the last judgment, and so God must know those saved from before all time and those condemned. What God knew remained God's business, he said; we should treat everyone as members of the elect.

Third, however, Reformed thinkers after Calvin prided themselves on the doctrine and sometimes said that predestination "showed" in people. This seems to me exactly the opposite of the point Jesus made about sheep and goats, when both groups of people seem surprised! At any rate, they did say that people could sometimes judge whether a person was predestined to glory or to destruction by observing God's care for that person on earth. Some passages from the Psalms, for example, supported such a claim. These theologians blew the doctrine of predestination out of proportion and said that belief in the doctrine was essential.

They also pictured God as impassive judge, a harsh portrait that invited John Wesley's rebuttal. Wesley, who started the Methodist movement in England and America, said that, first of all, God is love. He emphasized the Bible's teachings about prevenient grace, about Christian freedom, and about God's caring in mercy. Presbyterians frequently contrasted themselves with the Arminians, who said that God depended more on love than on eternal decrees in working out providence.

In the early twentieth century, two major Presbyterian bodies in the United States, the United Presbyterian Church U.S.A. and the Presbyterian Church U.S., took steps to make sure the doctrine was not overstated. They changed the standards under which they existed in order to speak of God's mercy and love. Presbyterians today can affirm Christian freedom, a compassionate God, and sound for all the world like Methodists if we wish.

We Presbyterians properly have kept reading the whole Bible. Our doctrines and our lifestyles are supposed to reflect that fact. And some of the teachings of Jesus, some of the Law and Prophets, Letters and Writings in the Bible do proclaim things that are difficult to hear. We therefore have a good reputation among Christians as people willing still to hear the "hard doctrines," that is, those about human judgment. A part of our source in this continuing effort to hear the "whole gospel" comes from attention to predestination.

These topics easily become more complicated. I have discovered this fact anew when I have tried to describe Calvinism, Arminianism, and the rest in encyclopedia articles. Interested

Presbyterians can turn to some of the good resources named in the section "For Further Study" (pages 115–18) to continue learning about our understandings of resurrection, predestination, and the like. We need now to look one more time at the whole fabric of faith together.

## Chapter Twelve

# To Grow in Grace

It is a bright, August Sunday morning at Williamsburg Presbyterian. Carolyn and I sit with the Matsushimas in the second row of chairs as the church school class of about forty adults studies Matthew 10. Today we are led by elder Larry Pulley, dean of the Mason School of Business Administration at the College of William and Mary. He shares leadership of the class with four others.

We read the passage together, in which Jesus gives instructions to the Twelve and sends them out: "See, I am sending you out like sheep into the midst of wolves; so be wise as serpents and innocent as doves" (Matt. 10:16).

Larry Pulley points to Jesus' sending disciples, named "apostles" here since they are "sent ones." They are not apprentices like those of the architect with whom Larry Pulley is working to construct the new business school building. Apostles do not have to get permission for every little thing. "No," he draws the contrast, "Jesus gives them authority to do exactly what he has been doing—proclaiming the kingdom of God, healing, raising the dead, cleansing lepers, casting out demons."

We discuss what Jesus' directions mean for us, for our witness and ministry. How can we proclaim the kingdom of God? How we can depend on "worthy houses" in which to reside, as Jesus told the apostles to find. Do we ever suffer for the gospel, as those apostles did?

We all try to understand the text and how it applies to our lives. Can Matthew 10 instruct us about growing in grace—being disciples and apostles? We work together to learn, bringing our different backgrounds and skills to the task. We listen carefully to one another.

After Sunday school, we join many others for morning worship, with hymns and prayers, Scripture readings, an offering, music, and a good sermon on Psalm 133, God's giving unity in the whole creation. God gives unity for our congregation's work and worship despite our diversity, the pastor proclaims.

I remember us also sitting in the pew with good friends at Anchorage, years ago. Associate pastor, Mary Morgan, read the Gospel lesson and preached. She reminded us of our tasks with the younger generations. "If our children come to church and hear one thing taught in Sunday school but see the institution functioning in a very different way," she warned, "chances are they will view Christianity as an hypocritical."

At Ginter Park Presbyterian in Richmond, Pastor Bob Pierce once talked about our responsibility to interpret for others how God's grace affects us. Numbers of us there would gather in Sunday school as well to learn about issues of peace and justice in our community. These are good memories of our family being informed and formed as Christians through the work and worship of congregations.

At Williamsburg we now congregate weekly in the parking lot after worship, exchanging news and asking about family among friends. Carolyn and I have done the same at every church we have attended. We also congregate on hayrides, in stewardship lunch meetings, in funeral parlors, at family night suppers, in committee meetings. With each congregation we have sought in many ways to learn and do the will of God. So have all the Christians with whom we have shared worship and work. Our church buildings may be old ones—have termites or smell like oranges. They may be new ones, mortgaged to the hilt. Our elders and pastors are not perfect either—failing to include young children in worship or slow to commit in mission. Still, we are Presbyterian churches going about our business, seriously and constructively, if never perfectly.

Our session representatives along with our ministers take part also in a presbytery and a regional synod. We are connected with and related to those in other congregations equally committed to serious and constructive work and worship. Through our benevolent gifts, we are tied even more broadly to Presbyterians and other Christians throughout the world—people who seek to bring the gospel to all nations. Through our prayers and acts of caring in every congregation, we are one with lots of other people and occasionally, mystically, even in tune sometimes with the whole of God's creation.

It is not easy to keep a big picture of the faith—to see some churches struggling to feed the hungry people in Ethiopia and see them as "us." It is hard to see a minister in Lesotho baptizing new Christians and ourselves as pledging to help nurture the converts. We have difficulty seeing Christians teaching in Japan and considering that part of our educational work or seeing British Christians building a television ministry and thinking of it as part of our mission. It is not easy to give up luxuries ourselves so that God's other children can have necessities for life. Nor is it a simple thing to try to follow Jesus in daily work, rearing children, or expecting God's kingdom to come on earth as in heaven. Yet we, the Presbyterian family of Christians, seek to do just those things. We aim to grow in grace, to worship God fully, and to "walk the walk while we talk the talk."

## Sanctification

I spoke earlier of the Holy Spirit as an agent of holiness. The work of holiness, of sanctification, seems to be counterintuitive much of the time. Objective observers of Reformed Christians who have not experienced the faith frequently comment on what they call an "irony" about us. How is it that Presbyterians and other Reformed Christians claim to believe in predestination, divine providence, the Holy Spirit giving all good things, and the failure of good works to help in salvation? Yet at the same time Reformed Christians have been and remain among the most intense workers in proclaiming the gospel and doing good deeds. How can these two things both be true?

We Presbyterians can answer quickly that we are just doing our Christian duty. The Reformed faith has no room for a "perfect Christian" in this life as the Holiness movement claims for itself. Nevertheless, we should work fervently in behalf of God's law and Christ's command. Jesus said, "If you love me, you will keep my commandments" (John 14:15). Can any Christian do less? By the same token, we affirm the "communion of saints" as firmly as Catholics, though we do not think anyone except Jesus can be a mediator between God and us. No one has a surplus of merit except Jesus.

Presbyterians still call the belief in God's Spirit enabling our good work "sanctification." The Larger Catechism, in one classic statement of doctrine, says:

> Sanctification is a work of God's grace, whereby they, whom God hath, before the foundation of the world, chosen to be holy, are, in time, through the powerful operation of his Spirit, applying the death and resurrection of Christ unto them, renewed in their whole man after the image of God; having the seeds of repentance unto life, and all other saving graces, put into their hearts, and those graces so stirred up, increased and strengthened, as that they more and more die unto sin, and rise into newness of life. (A.75)

There you have it—a compact statement of the meaning of sanctification, which is related to predestination, repentance, justification, and the power of the Spirit. Sanctification is the process by which we Christians integrate faith and work, but our fabric of living comes increasingly from God's Spirit.

What does sanctification mean? It means that we grow in grace. Gradually as we practice the discipline and faith, we are enabled to be better Christians. This is the kind of Christian life Paul prayed the Colossians would be able to live: "We have not ceased praying for you and asking that you may be filled with the

knowledge of God's will in all spiritual wisdom and understanding, so that you may lead lives worthy of the Lord, fully pleasing
to him, as you bear fruit in every good work and as you grow in
the knowledge of God" (Col. 1:9–10). Sanctification means that
our light shines, as we saw in chapter 5. But the purpose of it all,
according to Reformed faith, is not to make us good or perfect.
The purpose is to praise God, to render back in as good a life as
possible the gifts of the Spirit, the new life in Christ, which has
been given to us.

## Piety

Among Presbyterians the word is seldom used anymore, but
"piety" describes well the attitude of Reformed faith. It means
"reverence" and "devotion" to God. Historically, Presbyterians
have sought to make all of life an act of piety. Perhaps we do well
to remember some of the elements of this traditional lifestyle. Our
own tasks today may differ, and our worship styles may not be the
same, but we can learn from recalling the piety of other times.

In Presbyterian homes a hundred years ago, for example, the
whole family would gather nightly for Bible reading and prayer.
Some families are able still to engage in such a special time of
devotion daily, and others of us do it when complex schedules
allow. The saying of "blessings" regularly at meals and the reading of verses from the Bible are a part of this tradition, all acts of
piety, but also a part of Presbyterian piety historically has been
the commitment of an entire family to help people or groups in
need. Another part was the regular discussion of theology or values, so that younger Christians might learn why mature Christians did (or refrained from) certain activities.

At the turn of the twentieth century, Presbyterian denominations tried to make all member families engage in devotions
together. The institution of a "Family Altar" program, in which
persons had to report their piety, may have served to kill the vitality of it for many. As in many other things, Presbyterian piety has
differed among individuals, congregations, and denominations.
Many Presbyterians do not live in nuclear families, and piety

takes a variety of forms according to needs and opportunities. Notice, though, that such acts of devotion merely focus deeper, more profound reverence and devotion.

Many other aspects of Christian living for Presbyterians become acts of piety, not just the obvious things such as family devotions, personal devotions, refraining from commerce on Sunday when permitted, attending worship regularly, and being constant in prayer. I recall the piety of a carpenter who said he did the best job possible as an act of praise. At Anchorage Presbyterian Church, when the young people gathered on a Saturday to help an elderly woman clean her yard, it was an act of piety. When the drivers for Meals on Wheels take hot food to poor, shut-in people, they perform acts of devotion. When a businessperson seeks to be fair to all customers, he is demonstrating piety. When a physician stays with a member who is ill for a conversation to allay anxiety, she is demonstrating reverence for God. All of these actions, in the fabric of living to praise God, make sense together.

Piety is not just action, though. It also involves the inner life of the Christian. Piety is the love for God shared with a love for other people and for the whole creation. The grace of Christ, which enables prayer and devotion, forms the spiritual expression appropriate for the individual. Presbyterian piety in this realm is almost impossible to discuss, yet it has formed a significant part of being a Presbyterian and still does.

One way Reformed piety can be glimpsed is in reading the memoirs of and books about believers from previous generations. Presbyterians have relied on the very words of the Bible, especially those from the Psalms, as guides for their thinking about God during everyday life. They lived in the Psalms, so to say. Out of reading them and memorizing many of them, the psalms of Scripture became their window on God's relationship with their feelings and activities.

So for a mature Presbyterian a gorgeous day might suggest, "The heavens are telling the glory of God; and the firmament proclaims his handiwork" (Ps. 19:1). The beauty of the day would draw them through the words of a psalm to praise God. When times would be tough, that Presbyterian would think, "I lift up my eyes to the hills— from where will my help come? My help comes from the LORD, who made heaven and earth. He will not let your foot be moved" (Ps. 121:1–3). The worship service would remind the Presbyterian to "make a joyful noise to the LORD, all the earth" (Ps. 100:1). The meeting of a good friend could remind one to: "bless the LORD, O my soul; and all that is within me" (Ps. 103:1). Again an occasion for sin might be resisted as the mature Presbyterians recalled, "O LORD, you have searched me and known me. You know when I sit down and when I rise up; you discern my thought from far away" (Ps. 139:1–2). Gradually, imperceptibly, the mature Christian grows to "live in the Bible."

Notice that the discipline of studying the Psalms, the whole Bible, is involved. Notice that learning to hear the appropriate words from Scripture takes practice, too. Notice also how even this vehicle for practicing piety is not fully adequate. God's grace is given at every point in the Christian life. But here is one typical way in which Presbyterian piety has been exercised, in the actual authority of the Bible brought to bear on the events of daily life.

I guess my fear today is that we Presbyterians in exercising piety might be substituting little ways of praying and thinking for real, substantial living. What would we call the hollow saying of little prayers, or the emphasis on formal parts of praise? Piosity? Jesus said, "Whenever you pray, go into your room and shut the door and pray to your Father who is in secret" (Matt. 6:6). Presbyterian piety at its worst has sometimes made a show of righteous living and fancy praying. At its best, Presbyterian and Reformed piety has been quite full of real substance. It has been a way of life, and though aspects of it may differ among us with our various needs and gifts, it can be a way of life for us today too.

## Chapter Thirteen

# To Struggle in Faith and Humility

Right before Advent, right after Thanksgiving, comes Christ the King Sunday. Typically, the Scripture readings, the sermon, the prayers, and the hymns focus on the reign of Jesus Christ. So our choir belted out the joyful "Hallelujah" chorus from Handel's *Messiah*. Anthems in the Williamsburg church come during the collection of offerings. One by one, couple by couple, family by family, some members of the church did what they thought should be done when that chorus is played—stand!

The choir director smiled at the pastor, who almost laughed at the sight. Had either of them anticipated this? Young children passing the plates from pew to pew stopped in their tracks. And folks like Carolyn and me, who recognize that the tradition of standing is directly contrary to the force of the text and sermon, are caught wondering what to do. After all, King George II stood once as he left the hall during a performance more than 250 years ago, and those gathered in the royal audience were obliged to stand.

We had just heard that Jesus Christ is king—nobody else! Reluctantly, tardily, guiltily, we stood with our fellow worshipers. It was finally solidarity with our fellow worshipers that prevailed over doing what we thought was proper. I thought of the words of Paul to the believers in Corinth: "Take care that the liberty of yours does not somehow become a stumbling block to the weak"

(1 Cor. 8:9). Then I thought about my own arrogance, presuming to know better how to behave in worship than the fellow sinners alongside me. I was repentant and bemused at the same time.

Everyone standing surely made collecting the offering a unique and difficult experience. We made it through the chaos, but believe me, it was not a pretty sight!

What was going on? This confusion in a time of offering and choir singing is a symbol of the struggles and divisions that Presbyterians experience. This minor event in worship, doubtless forgotten by most in a few days, resembles more serious decisions and divisions Presbyterian congregations and governing bodies make all the time. New members and old elders alike need to be reminded that congregations (and wider Presbyterian bodies) struggle to do the right thing, to be faithful. In doing so, we stand with brothers and sisters even when our own opinions and sometimes even our convictions differ.

### A Presbyterian Congregation—A Big Tent

Time and again when I teach, Presbyterians ask about our differences within congregations, our conflicts, and especially our denominational stance on particular hot-button issues. It is possible in a small Presbyterian congregation for almost everyone to agree on most issues, especially a congregation in which a few farming families have gathered for generations. Any other Presbyterian congregation will have differences of opinion on many if not most public issues, even on many internal matters such as how we worship, how we practice the faith, and how we relate our Christian faith to that of other religions.

People come to Presbyterian churches for many reasons: they are invited by friends, they receive a service provided by that church, they hear that the pastor preaches well, they are new in town, they want to give their children "moral values" (as the man in Duluth), and so on. What they find either refreshes or repels them, based on how much they can tolerate differences in Christian worship and nurture. The hospitality of the church is important also, particularly when people listen to the visitors and invite them into real conversations and fellowship.

A student of "church growth" once said that Presbyterians debate too much and that the congregations usually "celebrate differences" rather than seeking homogeneity. That is a true observation from my experience. I think most who join Presbyterian congregations seek to grow and deepen their faith. They expect that people from a rather wide spectrum of educational and worship experiences will learn from and support one another well. They expect to learn and grow in some tension with others who are seeking to do the same.

## Thriving Congregations

Since I retired, I have been studying some Presbyterian congregations that thrive. How can I tell which are healthy? The task is actually simple enough. I listen to people talking about churches, visit many to preach and teach, and ask people, "How's your church doing?" If they respond with enthusiasm, I consider their church a healthy one.

There are a number of other marks of healthy churches too—members active in mission; a welcoming, hospitable atmosphere in worship and fellowship; and vital worship with good preaching, cheerful singing, and fervent prayers.

Thriving congregations are not afraid of differences in attitude, tension in allocating resources, and struggles to discern God's will. At one church where a permanent shelter for homeless people is in the building, I asked why the staff minced no words, why they spoke so directly and constructively to one another. "The clients at the shelter teach us honesty," the pastor told me. "We can talk straight with one another. As a result, our work is more effective." At another church where giving is particularly generous, members of the session explained that they regularly talk about stewardship of time and money.

At another congregation, a small one, that sponsors mission trips and projects in several countries overseas, I attended a meeting of the session. There church officers negotiated how many youth and adults they could take on mission efforts during the coming year. Some thought that taking as many youth as possible was the first priority. Another group sought to take people first who had never been on trips. Yet a third group wanted to mix youth and adults in both a domestic trip and one to another country. I sat amazed at their zeal and arguments, and I appreciated their final decision to give first choice to those who had never been on a trip, whether adults or young people.

The pastor later explained that she had trouble at first enlisting enough members for a mission trip. "Now they all want to go, and adults too."

"Can you find enough money to take the folks you decide to sponsor?" I asked.

"Sure," she replied. "Once we own the decision, we find the money rather quickly."

Out of the debate about priorities and selection of projects came mutual respect and a negotiated compromise that worked. Like the Corinthian dilemma concerning meat previously offered to idols, Paul found a personal compromise that favored the newer, more fragile believers (1 Cor. 8).

### From East, West, North, and South—<br>A Mainline Denomination

If a Presbyterian congregation is almost always a "big tent," with room for differences in opinion and style, the Presbyterian denomination is an even bigger one! Elders and pastors who have recently attended their first General Assembly (GA) come back to their congregations talking about the interesting variety of people there. A farmer from Nebraska, a homemaker from Georgia, a pastor from New York, a salesman from New Mexico, and about thirty other "commissioners" form each of the score or more "committees" to deal with overtures on a particular topic—evangelism or finances, for example. In selecting members of committees, denominational leaders try to put together people of different races, sexes, and age groups who are from congregations of various sizes. They try to get a representative group from the whole of the church throughout the country in order to be fair to all Presbyterians.

The committees meet together for days on end, opening their times of work with devotions, frequently breaking to sing hymns or pray. They become good friends working together—across geography, racial backgrounds, age differences, and sometimes opposite views on the matters they consider.

When the committees report, their recommendations are generally, though not always, accepted by the whole GA. Sometimes minority reports are made, with different recommendations. Sometimes the GA accepts the minority report, or maybe it will take parts of each report with a new amendment from the floor. The GA may take a stand on an issue, but it has limited authority and can always be reversed by another Assembly. The GA can also recommend changing the *Book of Order*, which requires a majority of presbyteries concurring to become effective. As I listen to the GA decisions, I hear them cast in humility rather than imperious tones. They "urge" more than they "require."

Such issues as ordaining women as elder and pastors, welcoming people of every race in all PCUSA churches, permitting pastors to celebrate marriage for people previously divorced, and offering Communion to children are examples of such stands taken in recent years.

Outside the hall where deliberations take place, people constantly picket and demonstrate, lobby and schmooze, all in an attempt to have their perspectives and points of view adopted.

This kind of national gathering is just one manifestation of a "mainline Protestant" denomination's life. It can be seen in the ongoing gatherings of the General Assembly Council, in which more than sixty men and women meet periodically throughout the year to carry forward decisions from the GA and other work of the denomination. They come from all over the country and try to act together for the good of the whole church.

Regional synods and presbyteries also carry forward the work of many congregations together, although much that used to happen in these "middle judicatories" is now accomplished by local congregations or single-interest organizations.

At one point, for example, the seminaries I served were "owned" by synods, supported especially to supply pastors and other church leaders in particular states and areas of the country. Today they answer to self-perpetuating boards of trustees, more as colleges do, rather than to synods. Today, with few exceptions, they are supported by congregations and individuals rather than by GA or middle judicatories. In Williamsburg Presbyterian Church, the congregation has responsibility for the campus ministry at the neighboring College of William and Mary. Campus ministry support used to come from GA, the Synod of Virginia, and the local presbytery.

The same is true for other churches in the American Protestant "mainline" traditions—whether Methodist, Episcopalian, Congregational, or Lutheran. All our strains of believing have been a part of life in towns, cities, and rural areas throughout the country for generations. Congregations in all these denominations also are changing as the culture changes and as life in the national bodies changes.

## Learning from Differences and Tension

I will never forget a Presbytery Day in Ohio, in which leaders and members from many churches gathered for worship, workshops, and fellowship. I was teaching a large class—about fifty Presbyterians—on our identity and mission. One middle-aged participant spoke out in discussion time: "And what is the Presbyterian stance on abortion?" Several other members of the group shared sideways smiles, knowing that this topic always produces heat as well as light in such a setting.

"Well," I began to explain, "the issue has been a live one for generations—especially since the *Roe v. Wade* decision of 1974 in the Supreme Court." I told of several study papers from the General Assembly and two books on the subject by prominent Presbyterians.

"In this very room next Tuesday," one woman offered, "the 'Presbyterians for Right to Life' will meet at 7:30 p.m. You are invited."

"Thursday night, down the street at First Church," another woman chimed in, "we pro-choice Presbyterians will be meeting. Please come join us."

"Oh," responded the questioner, "I just want to know the Presbyterian position on the issue."

At this point a friend in an adjacent chair gave the man a nudge and said, "Tell them where you came from and how long you have been a Presbyterian."

"I've been a Presbyterian for six months. I grew up Catholic."

The Catholic Church, the Southern Baptist Convention, many nondenominational community churches, and some others will tell their members what stance to take, even how to vote, on matters related to abortion. In these church bodies a pope, a preacher, or a gathering of preachers and others will demand that members of that church take a particular position on a public matter.

Presbyterians generally resent being told such things, though we do not mind being provided with resources—biblical, theological, scientific, and just plain insightful ones—that help us think clearly and come to mature positions.

On the issue of abortion, for example, some people are firmly convinced that terminating a pregnancy is murder, forbidden by the sixth commandment, "You shall not murder" (Exod. 20:13). With just as much conviction, others consider that it is more sinful to bring to life a baby that is not wanted or loved and has little chance of being nurtured to trust and be happy. This is particularly so if the pregnancy is the result of rape or is jeopardizing the health of the mother. Presbyterian GAs have recently sided more with the second position than the first. Primarily, however, the church offers study papers and simply refuses to declare abortion necessarily a greater sin than its alternatives.

To take another issue, many opponents of ordaining practicing homosexuals believe the Bible strictly prohibits homosexual relations, while others equally serious read the Bible differently and consider it a matter of justice to place in responsible positions men and women capable of ministry rather than judging their personal predilections. In both cases, it should be quickly stated, many Presbyterians see the biblical authority, logic, and ethics of both, contrasting stances.

These opposing positions are matters of significance, and there are numbers of other such issues that divide Presbyterians empowered by the Holy Spirit and trying to follow Jesus.

## Worship, Learning, Care, Fellowship, and Mission

What is the purpose of a Presbyterian congregation anyhow? Those who study congregations point out that the main functions of a congregation are religious—worship of God, learning together, caring for one another and others, fellowship, and mission in the name of Jesus Christ. Though congregations sometimes advocate certain perspectives politically and socially, if one focuses too much on such goals, it becomes just another nonprofit. On the other hand, as we have seen time and again, if congregations focus on worship and praise of God, on learning together a Christian way of life, they cannot be content just serving themselves. They reach out to others in mission and proclamation of the joy in Christ.

The more Presbyterians mature, the less defensive we become. In the healthy congregations I have studied, members and officers are quick to see their own shortcomings, quick to ask about the ways others are engaged in faithful work and worship, and modest about their own attainments.

One focus for most healthy congregations now is their efforts to incorporate Christian practices from their Reformed heritage and from other branches of the family of faith. That topic also deserves some attention.

## Chapter Fourteen

# To Practice the Faith

A t least for several years, a "Bread Ministry" provided hospitality. First-time visitors to Sunday worship at Ginter Park Presbyterian Church received a loaf of freshly baked bread at their doorstep that afternoon, with a friendly note inviting them back. The church member knocked on their door and conversed briefly if the visitor wanted to learn more about the church.

At the Williamsburg church, we practice hospitality as elders and other congregational leaders speak warmly to welcome visitors—sometimes many of them, who come to Colonial Williamsburg from all over the country. Each Sunday a worship leader invites people thinking about membership to speak with a pastor. A coffee time hosted by various families and individuals permits visitors to receive refreshments and conversation with longtime members.

In the Anchorage church, as many members of the Session as possible would attend the funeral of a member. Elders sit together for the "Witness to the Resurrection," and they organize a reception afterward if requested so members of the family can receive condolences at the church.

At every church I have attended, people plan and provide many kinds of educational experiences for members of the church and others on Sundays. Every congregation also offers opportunities for members to give time, expertise, and money for those in need.

In every congregation, a choir sings to praise God. Though some congregations seem more reluctant to sing their faith, others embrace with enthusiasm the practice of singing. Each church sings both old favorites and newer hymns in worship.

These practices—hospitality, dying well, studying together, and singing the faith—are just some of the many maintained in Presbyterian congregations. Children in the congregation learn some of the practices before they learn to speak about their beliefs. New adult Christians as well frequently attend worship or church school, sing and give, experience forgiveness and prayer, before they understand much of what Presbyterians believe. In fact, it is worth considering whether Reformed Christianity is first and foremost a way of living more than it is a particular theological flavor. This expanded edition of *To Be a Presbyterian* permits some concerted attention to Presbyterian practices, most of which we hold in common with the rest of the Christian family, but some of which are distinctive among the Reformed.

## The Range of Christian Practices

Since this book's original edition in 1983, much has been learned and taught about Christian practices—concrete human acts that are done together and over time in the name of Jesus Christ. It behooves Presbyterians to consider the ways in which we embody our beliefs. In the first edition, there were sections and chapters on some practices—Sabbath observance, prayer, giving generously, and forgiveness, for example—and those sections have been expanded somewhat in this revision.

After that book came out, Christian practices in every part of the church have received concerted attention. The Valparaiso Project has identified twelve Christian spiritual disciplines, and phrases quoted are from the book that began a whole series on the subject—*Practicing Our Faith*, edited by Dorothy Bass (1997).

> Honoring the body—paying attention to your own body and the body of every other person as a "temple of the Holy Spirit" (1 Cor. 6:19).

Hospitality—offering cordial and generous welcome to people, especially those in need.

Household economics—"arranging what is necessary" for the well-being of the family, living appropriately, and caring that others are able to do so.

Saying yes and saying no—affirming life-giving ways of living and avoiding destructive ones.

Keeping Sabbath—stopping the daily toil regularly to praise God and refresh the spirit.

Testimony—publicly telling of God's care and one's personal faith.

Discernment—seeking God's will in community and as individuals.

Shaping communities—helping "good governance and able leadership" emerge to foster healthy communities for faith and life.

Forgiveness—feelings, words, and actions that help restore communities and personal relationships.

Healing—seeking wholeness for people and communities through prayer, prevention of illnesses, skilled intervention, and medical care.

Dying well—seeking to praise God as we move toward death and providing solidarity with those in grief at the death of another.

Singing our faith—praising God in hymns and songs in worship and life more broadly.

## Prayer and Practices

Although we certainly engage regularly in prayer, both individually and together in congregations and other gatherings, most who study Christian practices claim that it underlies all of them. Prayer permits discernment, for example, and it gives deep meaning to hymns we sing in faith. The Holy Spirit makes our words and deeper groans into prayers—communication with God through Christ. Disciplined prayer has certainly been a part of Christian practice since the inception of the church.

John Calvin advised believers to pray at least six times every day—especially at meals, at rising, and at bedtime. All of us who pray frequently know that we are not kept from it by our own situation or the presence of others. Prayer can take place in our hearts with no words uttered, with no hands raised, and with no head bowed. Prayers can be instantaneous, prolonged, or anywhere in between. We can pray with others or by ourselves.

We can pray to become more proficient in each of these practices—to be more hospitable, to be more forgiving, to be constructive in building communities and shaping them according to God's will.

## Special Presbyterian Practices

On almost every occasion in which I study practices with groups or classes of Presbyterians, someone will give an illustration of a member of the congregation especially focused on "saying yes and saying no," someone disciplined over the years to live modestly and who is full of generosity. Presbyterians are not the only Christians proficient in this practice, but many are very experienced. The things of this world mean little in comparison with the higher values and goals for life. This part of the "Presbyterian way" may also be considered as a "household economics" practice as well.

At Louisville Seminary, where I served for many years, I kept asking a member of Grace Hope Presbyterian to speak to students and other lay leaders in congregations on stewardship. A mailman for forty years and among the early African Americans permitted to deliver mail throughout town, he had begun tithing from the time he was first employed. He told of stewardship in his family, where children learned early about giving, of saving to buy a house so rent money would not "go down the drain," and of trying to help others in the church think about giving and sharing talents. Now in his retirement, he was sharing expertise with others—a mature theology of using God's gifts wisely.

Another Presbyterian in that city, who belonged to a small downtown congregation, came to see us. He wore an old suit and an even older tie, and in conversation he told us in a confessional style that now he "treated" his wife and himself as he had not done previously. They went to lunch most Sundays at a Denny's restaurant—a nice but comparatively inexpensive place to eat.

He also told us he wanted to endow a prize to reward people who helped others progress in their understanding about God, God's work, and God's care. Soon he gave several million dollars to our seminary and the local university to offer prizes in religion, music, ethics, and other human endeavors. He said no to living a fancy life in order to be able to say yes to rewarding others for humane achievements.

In Richmond there is a woman who succeeded nicely in the antiques business, but she passed the work to others in order to concentrate on helping ex-convicts become useful members of society—teaching them to refinish antiques, help people move furniture, and run businesses themselves. She said no to making more money in order to say yes to meeting the needs of others, in this case people with whom Jesus was particularly concerned—those in prison.

When I served as a seminary president, I would go to see Presbyterians in various cities throughout the country, people who might contribute to help educate pastors and teachers for the future of the church. Almost invariably I would be directed to stop at "the smallest house on the block," or told, "Don't be surprised by the appearance" of a donor or a potential donor.

At the Anchorage church, one elder always wore a T-shirt with a slogan—"Have You Hugged a Teacher Today?" or "Your Library Support Is Overdue." This former superintendent of public instruction for the state of Kentucky said he wore T-shirts because he "wanted everyone to be welcome at church." He said no to fashion in order to practice exceptional hospitality to strangers, guests, and the poor.

A sociologist looking at Reformed Christians some time ago said we engage in "this-worldly asceticism," denying ourselves immediate luxuries to engage in longer-term efforts based on our values and faith. And the scholars who explain the practices remind us that *askēsis*, the Greek root of "asceticism," means "discipline" or "training."

We are not the only Christians who engage in frugal lifestyles, but we may be alone in mentioning such a practice in our Form of Government. As a major theme of the Reformed tradition, we claim that we try to practice "a faithful stewardship that shuns ostentation and seeks proper use of the gifts of God's creation" (G-2.0500a[3]).

## The Practice of Study

Most Christians study, but it seems to me that Presbyterians are particularly adept at this practice, which is not listed by the Valparaiso Project. We study the Bible. We study social issues. We study to become proficient in various professions. We study simply to learn all the marvelous things we can know.

Look around in your congregation and you will probably find most people caring about study of some kind. Disproportionate numbers of teachers and librarians among our members give one indication of our love for study. Care for what people are reading is another.

As we saw in chapter 7, as Reformed Christianity spread through Europe, the literacy rates among those populations skyrocketed, especially the proportions of readers among women and girls. The same is true for newer Presbyterian and Reformed churches in emerging nations.

Some years ago, when assigned to a group of scholars studying "postdenominational America," I asked, "Is there a special Presbyterian culture?" to leaders across the denomination. They replied to a person that indeed there is a discernible one—for Presbyterians are people of the "Word." "If there is a misspelling in the bulletin," one told me, "people will pay attention to it." When I asked another if that were true, she replied, "Yes. Sometimes I think Presbyterians pay more attention to the spelling and grammar than to the substance of the message."

Their lighthearted evidence of a Presbyterian culture rings true in congregations where I have belonged and where I have visited. We do pay extraordinary attention to study of various sorts, and we care about words and writing.

Frequently our lives are so formed by study, our values so unconsciously embody this practice of study that we do not even attribute it to our faith. Some years ago, when I sought to write on the study papers of Presbyterian denominations and synods, I discovered the topic to be so complex and huge that I soon despaired. By comparison, a colleague in another Protestant denomination wrote a medium-sized book that outlined rather well all the stances of that communion over the twentieth century. She told me that she estimated the Presbyterian church had forty study papers and stands for each one written by her denomination.

I do not imagine that the Presbyterian predilection for the study of things is superior or inferior when compared to the inclinations of others. I simply note our propensity to engage deeply in the practice of study.

### Learning Practices from Other Christians

Yet another benefit of our current situation, in which new Presbyterians are coming from diverse backgrounds, is that we can learn from the heritage of others. In a congregation in Burnsville, North Carolina, I saw in the Sunday bulletin an insert titled "The Privileges of Children Here in Worship." It spoke of the rights of young ones to be "in the midst of the congregation, not on the sidelines; to wander among us during worship, being the responsibility of each of us; and to be called by name by each adult." When I asked how they came to this, the pastor responded that parents who had grown up Mennonites had suggested it. Mennonites are particularly attuned to the practices of household economics and hospitality. Having members who prized those practices helped teach them among Presbyterians. (And the Burnsville Presbyterian Church was full of families with small children!)

In a Presbyterian congregation in Harrisonburg, Virginia, there were highly functioning small groups and diverse mission emphases resembling those of much larger congregations. I learned that they model their life together on practices in an ecumenical congregation in nearby Washington, D.C., with high expectations of members.

Presbyterians coming from Lutheran backgrounds are particularly knowledgeable about and devoted to theological education. Former Episcopalians may well have been participants in excellent marriage enrichment programs that permeate portions of that denomination. Former Methodists may have special knowledge of relationships with churches in other lands. Christian immigrants from Africa may know how to "dance the offering," a joyful living out of generosity.

And, of course, the word "practice" itself functions as a verb in addition to its service as a noun. So like the old saw about getting to Carnegie Hall, practice might be useful in thinking about becoming a Presbyterian.

Students of Reformed practices might attempt to be proficient Presbyterians by practicing.

## Chapter Fifteen

# To Enjoy God Forever

A s we come into the sanctuary at the Williamsburg Presbyterian Church in early March, we are greeted by college students serving as ushers. It reminds us that today is "WESFEL
Sunday," the day on which students in the Westminster Fellowship at the neighboring College of William and Mary take responsibility for preaching, selecting the hymns, anthems, prayers, and
even making the announcements. As a congregation, we enjoy
this ministry and have even kept our crowded location as the
church has grown, sacrificing adequate parking to be near the
college and its students. We thoroughly enjoy the participation
and the talents of the young people.

A number of the students participate in a bell choir, and their
disciplined ringing of different kinds of bells makes a joyful noise
indeed! We enjoy the spirit of the student ushers, the varied voices
of those who read Scripture lessons and lead us in prayers. We
enjoy hearing not one but two sermons—both focused on God's
gift of faith and our discernment through life of vocation and
mission. We consider what their leadership means and will mean
for decades to come in Presbyterian churches and elsewhere.

The sermons challenge us to grow in trust of God, to be agents
of peace and justice, to take up our crosses as Jesus told his disciples to do. Youthful enthusiasm, good insights, and idealism

abound. The whole experience is fun—worship led by those who are at once the present and the future of the church.

Seeing and hearing the young students brings a lump to my throat and quickens my soul. It makes me thankful that our church is assisting in this ministry. It reminds me that I should be more generous in giving time, talents, and money for this crucial work. The students' presence and leadership remind me that Presbyterian congregations need to cultivate young leaders and pray for them. Finally, witnessing these young people reminds me that our goal—the end for all of us—is to glorify God and enjoy God forever.

### Enjoy God Forever

The two catechisms from our confessional standards—the Shorter and the Larger Westminster Catechisms—both begin with same question: "What is the chief end of man?" (Of course, the word "man" was in the 1640s assumed to include "woman," as for some Presbyterians it still does.) The writers of the two catechisms were not trying to be cute, and no other questions and answers are exact duplicates in both standards. In fact, the end or goal is this simple for Presbyterians. Sometimes when I get all wrapped up in trying to understand or to explain a belief or a practice, or when I get frustrated about the problems in our church, I stop to remind myself that we are just human beings blessed with amazing mysteries and amazing grace to glimpse them at all. Thank God!

The first answer also is identical in both catechisms: "Man's chief end is to glorify God and enjoy him forever." This succinct expression of Reformed faith comes straight from the Bible. In this case, a psalmist sings to God, "Nevertheless, I am continually with you; you hold my right hand. You guide me with your counsel, and afterward you will receive me with honor" (Ps. 73:23–24). According to John's Gospel, Jesus prayed that God would grant believers presence with him: "Father, I desire that those also, whom you have given me, may be with me where I am, to see my glory, which you have given me because you loved me before the foundation of the world" (John 17:24). Perhaps most directly, Paul told the Corinthians to glorify God in everything: "So, whether you eat or drink, or whatever you do, do everything for the glory of God" (1 Cor. 10:31).

## My Prayer for Presbyterians

In recent years as I have taught Presbyterians and written books and letters, I have been drawn to make very personal pleas and prayers in behalf of readers and colleagues in the faith. It makes sense at this point to conclude with words of my pleas and prayers for you who seek to be faithful Presbyterians, or even for those just considering what Presbyterians believe.

I ask that you remember and enjoy your participation in the whole Christian family—those throughout the world today and those who faithfully have completed their race in previous generations and cheer us on from the heavenly balcony. I ask that you enjoy participation in the Christian journey, the Spirit-guided race to grow in Jesus Christ.

I ask that you grow in trust—especially in faith that God is God of all life and death and resurrection. We all have times of doubt. But gradually, imperceptibly, those doubts are diminished and trust is increased as we pray, as we engage others in the Christian practices, and as we study from books and from the lives of others what it means to follow Jesus.

I ask that you seek to grow in love—for others, for yourself, for your congregation and the wider church, and for God's creation. Naturally, you will love God more as you come to love God's handiwork.

To God I pray that you will given heaping measures of faith, hope, and love. I pray that you will be guided and guarded by the work of the Holy Spirit, sanctified as you continue in discipleship.

I pray you will be given better vision as time goes—to see ever more of the human family as our neighbor. We hear time and again that the earth is growing smaller (and flatter, for that matter). We can extend the proclamation of the gospel in loving our neighbors as ourselves.

I pray that you will be granted the special gift to see the glorious truth and nourishment for us in baptisms and times of celebrating the Lord's Supper. In fact, I pray that you will find sacred meaning also in much of your family life and congregational life, in your life as a good citizen and a decent human being. I pray that you will perceive God's work—the Holy Spirit's work—as children learn to sing the faith and as you witness people "dying well" in the faith.

I pray that you have found or will find ways to exercise your particular Christian vocation, doing things you enjoy and doing them well for the glory of God. Equally, I pray that you will support and encourage others in living out their vocations well.

I pray that you will grow increasingly to anticipate God's kingdom coming on earth as it is in heaven, glimpse it dawning, and yearn for it to blossom fully.

Finally, I pray that you will glorify God and enjoy God, both personally and together with others in your church and more broadly in the world. Amen.

# For Further Study

This book has offered a brief introduction to congregational life in the Presbyterian Church (U.S.A.). I hope that now you will want to read and think, pray and study more about the Christian faith and about your experience within it. The place to begin is with the Bible. Many translations are available now, with different costs and benefits in using each. I rely on the New Revised Standard Version and the New English Bible especially, but I still employ the King James Version to refresh my memory for passages I memorized as a child.

The *Book of Order* and the *Book of Confessions* of the Presbyterian Church (U.S.A.) are updated from time to time. A recent copy of both will be extremely helpful, and a study edition of the *Book of Confessions* explains the setting of each statement of faith.

Here are a few of the many books especially for Presbyterians that can offer next steps in learning about ourselves, our history, our practices, and our witness.

## Brief studies of the Presbyterians

Davidson, James E. *The Living Water: A Guide to Baptism for Presbyterians.* Louisville, KY: Westminster John Knox Press, 2000). This down-to-earth book shows reasons for baptism and responsibilities of those who baptize Presbyterians.

Gear, Felix. *Our Presbyterian Belief.* Atlanta: John Knox Press, 1980. Speaks about basic doctrine in a simple fashion.

Lingle, Walter, and John Kuykendall. *Presbyterians, Their History and Beliefs.* Atlanta: John Knox Press, 1978. Particularly good as a study book for groups and church school classes looking at both theology and history especially of "Southern" Presbyterians.

Loetscher, Lefferts A. *A Brief History of the Presbyterians.* 4th ed., with a new chapter by George Laird Hunt. Philadelphia: Westminster Press, 1983. Concentrates on the "Northern" Presbyterians, though it also treats the "Southern" and other branches.

McKim, Donald K. *Introducing the Reformed Faith: Biblical Revelation, Christian Tradition, Contemporary Significance.* Louisville, KY: Westminster John Knox Press, 2001. Includes clear sections on each topic for advanced beginners.

———. *Presbyterian Beliefs: A Brief Introduction.* Louisville, KY: Geneva Press, 2003. Another introduction—a simple one for beginners.

———. *Presbyterian Questions, Presbyterian Answers: Exploring Christian Faith.* Louisville, KY: Geneva Press, 2004. A guide in catechism form.

Rogers, Jack. *Presbyterian Creeds: A Guide to the Book of Confessions.* Philadelphia: Westminster Press, 1985. An explanation of the contexts for the writing of the creeds and statements of faith we affirm.

Smylie, James H. *A Brief History of the Presbyterians.* Louisville, KY: Geneva Press, 1996. This well-written classic concentrates nicely on the balance between the different streams of American Presbyterianism.

Weeks, Louis B. *The Presbyterian Source: Bible Words That Shape a Faith.* Louisville, KY: Westminster/John Knox Press, 1990. Focuses on some biblical passages that have been formative for Presbyterian practice, governmental structure, and theology. Follows the history of Presbyterian practice and belief in light of biblical roots.

## More Thorough Studies of Presbyterians in America

Coalter, Milton J, and Virgil Cruz, eds. *How Shall We Witness: Faithful Evangelism in a Reformed Tradition.* Louisville, KY: Westminster John Knox Press, 1995. Essays on conversion, the gospel, awakenings, outreach, social witness and evangelism, and theology of evangelism for Presbyterians.

Loetscher, Lefferts A. *The Broadening Church: A Study of Theological Issues in the Presbyterian Church since 1869.* Philadelphia: University of Pennsylvania Press, 1954. Explores the fundamentalist movement and its impact on Presbyterians.

McKim, Donald, ed. *The Westminster Handbook to Reformed Theology.* Louisville, KY: Westminster John Knox Press, 2001. Provides dictionary-style articles on all major beliefs.

McNeill, John T. *The History and Character of Calvinism.* New York: Oxford University Press, 1960. Perhaps the best overall guide to Presbyterian theology and history, including Reformed life in many different cultures.

Sundquist, Scott, and Caroline Becker, eds. *A History of Presbyterian Missions, 1944–2007.* Louisville, KY: Geneva Press, 2008. Excellent treatment of Presbyterian partnerships and mission in many countries.

Thompson, Ernest Trice. *Presbyterians in the South.* 3 vols. Atlanta: John Knox Press, 1963–1973. Comprehensive tracing of the roots and extent of Southern Presbyterian life until immediately before the merger with the UPCUSA.

Thompson, Robert E. *A History of the Presbyterian Churches in the United States.* American Church History Series, Vol. 6. New York: Christian Literature, 1895, and several reprints. This classic study of Northern Presbyterians is still helpful.

Trinterud, Leonard. *The Forming of an American Tradition.* Philadelphia: Westminster Press, 1970. Documents the beginning of the first, unique Presbyterian denomination in the new United States from many ethnic sources and several strains of Reformed theology.

Wallace, Dewey. *Puritans and Predestination: Grace in English Protestant Theology.* Chapel Hill: University of North Carolina Press, 1982. A good treatment of a strain of predestinarian thought.

Weeks, Louis. "Presbyterianism." Pages 499–510 in *Encyclopedia of the American Religious Experience*, vol. 1, ed. Charles H. Lippy and Peter W. Williams. New York: Charles Scribner's Sons, 1988.

## The Comprehensive Study of the Presbyterian Church

Coalter, Milton J., John M. Mulder, and Louis B. Weeks, eds. *The Presbyterian Presence: The Twentieth Century Experience.* 7 vols. Louisville, KY: Westminster/John Knox Press, 1990–1992. Titles for each volume are listed below:

> *The Confessional Mosaic: Presbyterians and Twentieth-Century Theology* (1990)
>
> *The Diversity of Discipleship: Presbyterians and Twentieth-Century Witness* (1991)
>
> *The Mainstream Protestant "Decline": The Presbyterian Pattern* (1990)
>
> *The Organizational Revolution: Presbyterians and American Denominationalism* (1992)
>
> *The Presbyterian Predicament: Six Perspectives* (1990)
>
> *The Pluralistic Vision: Presbyterians and Mainstream Protestant Education and Leadership* (1992)
>
> *The Re-Forming Tradition: Presbyterians and Mainstream Protestantism* (1992)

## Studies on Christian, Protestant, and Presbyterian Practices

Bass, Dorothy C., ed. *Practicing Our Faith: A Way of Life for a Searching People.* San Francisco: Jossey-Bass, 1997. Includes contributions from several Presbyterians.

Bass, Dorothy C., and Craig Dykstra, eds. *For Life Abundant: Practical Theology, Theological Education, and Christian Ministry.* Grand Rapids: Wm. B. Eerdmans Publishing Co., 2008. This more complex study relates practices to practical theology.

Bass, Dorothy C., and Don C. Richter, eds. *Way to Live: Christian Practices for Teens.* Nashville: Upper Room Books, 2002. This adaptation of the practices is for younger Christians.